The Johannine Writings
By Paul W. Schmiedel
Edited by Anthony Uyl

Devoted Publishing
Woodstock, Ontario, 2017

The Johannine Writings
By Paul W. Schmiedel (1851-1935)
Professor of Theology at Zurich
Translated by Maurice A. Canney, M.A.
Edited by Anthony Uyl

London; Adam and Charles Black; 1908

The text of The Johannine Writings is all in the Public Domain. This edition is published by Devoted Publishing a division of 2165467 Ontario Inc.

What kind of philosophies do you have?
Let us know!

Contact us at: devotedpub@hotmail.com
Visit our shop on Facebook: @DevotedPublishing
Published in Woodstock, Ontario, Canada 2017

For bulk educational rates, please contact us at the above email address.

ISBN: 978-1-77356-018-2

Table of Contents

PREFACE

IN the German edition, the present work comprises three parts (8, 10, and 12) of the well-known "Religionsgeschichtliche Volksbücher." The present edition gathers these discussions of the Johannine (and incidentally of the Synoptic) problem into a single volume. It has the further advantage--through the kindness of Prof. Schmiedel--of incorporating many manuscript improvements in and additions to the German text. For instance--not to mention smaller additions--§§ 26 and 27 in Pt. I. Chap. III. (pp. 130-136), the second and third paragraphs of § 13 in Pt. II. Chap. V. (pp. 255-257), and the second note in the Appendix (pp. 270-277) are entirely new. In fact, in this, as in other matters, Prof. Schmiedel has spared himself no trouble in order to lay the results of his studies in as complete a form as possible (having regard, of course, to the limitations imposed by a popular German series) before his English readers. In the List of Books at the end of the volume references will be found to some of the author's contributions to the "Encyclopaedia Biblica "which bear directly upon the subject under consideration. It is hoped that the present work will serve as an introduction, and in some respects as a supplement, to Prof. Schmiedel's famous "Encyclopaedia" articles.

THE TRANSLATOR.
July 1908.

Paul W. Schmiedel

PART I - THE FOURTH GOSPEL IN COMPARISON WITH THE FIRST THREE GOSPELS

INTRODUCTION

THOSE whose knowledge of the Life of Jesus has been acquired merely from Religious Instruction or from attendance at church services, or from a "Bible History" designed for use in schools, do not realise how much of it is based entirely upon the Fourth Gospel. If we did not possess this, we should know nothing at all about the marriage-feast at Cana, about the cure of the sick man who had lain for thirty-eight years by the Pool of Bethesda, about the gift of sight to the man who was born blind, about the raising of Lazarus, about the washing of the disciples' feet on the last evening of Jesus' life, and about the spear being thrust into the side of the crucified Lord. As regards the expulsion of the dealers and money-changers from the fore court of the Temple, our knowledge would be to the effect that it happened not at the beginning, but at the end, of Jesus' public ministry. Of Jesus' capture we should only have the report that it was effected by a band of armed men despatched by the Jewish authorities, not that it was carried out by the Roman soldiers. The day of Jesus' death would be known to us as the day after, not the day before, the evening on which the Jews ate the paschal lamb. In the case of the crucifixion of Jesus, we should know no more than that, of all his followers, only a number of women looked on from a distance; we should not be aware that his mother and his beloved disciple stood by the cross and received a message from his lips.

These few observations are sufficient in themselves to give us pause to think. Why do the first three Evangelists tell us nothing of all that the Fourth is able to report? Did these things not come within the range of their experience? Yet at most of the events we have mentioned all those are reported to have been present who after wards became apostles; about the others also they must have received very soon afterwards quite definite information, and through them in due course, or through intermediaries, the authors of our Gospels. Or can it be that they had some reason for passing over the information in question? And yet how gladly would they have incorporated it in their books! This same information would surely have served the purpose which they had in view in the whole of their literary undertaking-- that of making the figure of their Master shine forth in the brightest light--better almost than all that they have included in their narratives!

Why then did they not introduce it? Did they really have no experience of these episodes, though not indeed because they did not happen? We cannot avoid the question. Nor can we dispose of it off-hand, either in the affirmative or in the negative, by a few considerations. Nothing but a general review of the differences between the Fourth Gospel and the first three will enable us to supply the answer. And, first, these differences must be determined without any prepossessions whatever in favour of one or the other story; secondly, attempts to reconcile the two accounts, in spite of their divergences, must be made and tested; and then only after such attempts have failed shall we be called upon to decide definitely which of the two is the more trustworthy.

We say more trustworthy. The obvious thing to say would seem to be, Which account deserves to be trusted altogether? But that would not only be unwise for general reasons--because, for instance, an untrustworthy account is not always the necessary alternative to a thoroughly trustworthy one--but also because the matter is not really presented to us in this way. Should the scales turn in favour of the first three Gospels, we are still obliged to bear in mind continually such evidence as that produced by Wernle, for example, in the first number of this series (Religionsgeschichtliche Volksbücher), concerning the Sources for the Life of Jesus, which shows that none of these was composed by a man who saw Jesus' ministry with his own eyes, and that their trustworthiness is subject to considerable limitations. If the Fourth Gospel deserve preference, its author would certainly appear to have been an eyewitness of the work of Jesus. But even then the possibility arises--and those who accept this view fully avail themselves of it--that in his recollection of events much of his material became dislocated or was more or less seriously obscured.

After comparing the Fourth Gospel with the first three as regards its trustworthiness, our study must advance to an ever wider investigation of its peculiar character, and must then bring to light its deeper roots in the conceptions and ideas prevailing at the time. Later, in Part II. of the present work, we shall have to come to some conclusion as to the author, and the time in which this book and the writings related to it--all supposed to have been written by the same Apostle John--were composed. Finally, we shall have to show the abiding value of these works. Thus, at first we have to enter upon an enumeration of those special points in which the Fourth Gospel differs from the other three. This enumeration might easily be thought a somewhat external matter. The task, however, cannot be avoided because it is of primary importance to find our general bearings. Only gradually can the special peculiarities of the book from higher points of view be summed up in such a way as to present consistent pictures. As regards each particular narrative of the Gospel, therefore, we cannot say at once all that is to be said about it. On the contrary, many narratives will come up for discussion in very many places, our purpose being to show at each stage of our inquiry some new phase which helps to elucidate the question under consideration.

But, on the whole, we are concerned with nothing less than the question, What picture ought we ourselves to form of Jesus? The Fourth Gospel sketches the picture in a very pronounced and quite peculiar way, and no one can pass on without deciding for or against it. The main question with regard to this is whether its features accord with the figure of Jesus as he really existed upon earth, or whether such have been added as were derived from a different, and perhaps even a non-Christian, type of piety and view of the world. Here we have the reasons for including in the present series of books on the history of religion a particularly detailed, treatment of this remarkable book, which has already been called the most wonderful riddle--that is to say, the riddle most replete with what is inconceivable--of all the books of the New Testament.

Turning now to our actual investigation, in accordance with general usage we shall gladly retain the name John (shortened to Jn.) to describe the author, just as in the case of the three other Evangelists we keep the names Matthew (Mt.), Mark (Mk.), Luke (Lk.). Strictly speaking, we should have always to put these names in quotation marks; but that would certainly prove wearisome. Mt., Mk., and Lk. have received in scientific theology the common name "Synoptics," because their gospels, in virtue of their far-reaching agreement, may be regarded or "viewed together" with one glance (Synopsis means "common view"). But even as regards this, it will be borne in mind that the agreement is by no means complete. Only on the whole, and only in comparison with Jn., is it apparent. Where it is found on a particular point, for the sake of simplicity we shall refer only to the Evangelist who gives what is presumably the most original form of a report, that is to say in most cases (though not always) Mk., as representing that which appears in all three Synoptics, Mt. being referred to mostly for those discourses of Jesus not preserved in Mk., or given by Mk. in a less original form. From Lk., therefore, for the most part, only such sections will be cited as are not found in Mk. and Mt.

The parallel passages from the other Gospels, which we do not quote, will be found on the margin of most Bibles, either by the side of the verse itself which forms part of a discourse, or at the head of a section to which it belongs. In a more convenient form they may be seen at a glance in a "Synopsis," where they are always printed side by side (see the appended list of books). In addition, however, a copy of the New Testament will be indispensable, because, as one can easily understand, in a Synopsis the context in which a passage stands in the Gospel of which it forms part is not always clear.

At the least, it seems to us to be a matter of urgent necessity that the reader should have a New Testament by his side. Nothing could be further from our wishes than that people should be prepared, or think themselves condemned, to believe our assertions without testing them. And yet it is not possible always to print the whole section of the Bible on which they are based.

By inserting the number of the chapters and verses in the text of this book, we shall, we believe, be studying the reader's convenience better than by giving the references at the foot of the page or at the end of the work. Those who are not interested in them will not, we hope, allow themselves to be distracted by them or think that for their own convenience they should have been omitted altogether, but will be prepared to pass over them. There are some readers--and we hope they are many--who will wish to turn them up, and it may even happen that one of those who in the first instance has felt the numbers to be distracting will suddenly have to be included in the other class of readers. If we had done as he at first wished he would now find himself obliged to search rather helplessly in a Bible with which he is perhaps not very familiar.--An f. after a verse-number refers only to the following verse. [1]

Footnote:

1. The headings to the subdivisions of chapters were added after the book was already in print, to make it more convenient for readers to use. Consequently, the first words of a new section often follow immediately upon the last words of the preceding section without any regard to the heading.

CHAPTER I - THE DIFFERENCE BETWEEN THE FIRST THREE GOSPELS AND THE FOURTH

1. DURATION OF JESUS MINISTRY.

ONE of the first points on which one wishes to be clear, if one would obtain a general view of the stories of Jesus' life, is this--How long did Jesus' public ministry last? As regards this, Jn. gives us information which is quite clear. The expulsion of the dealers and money-changers from the fore-court of the Temple, which was only preceded by the presence of Jesus at the marriage feast at Cana in Galilee, took place when Jesus had gone up (ii. 13) to Jerusalem to keep the Passover feast, our Easter Festival. Shortly before a second Passover festival, in Galilee by the Lake of Gennesareth he fed the five thousand (vi. 4). At a third Passover feast (xi. 55; xii. 1; xiii. 1) Jesus met his death. Between these there is mention of three other feasts. Between the first and second Passover, a "feast of the Jews," which is not more closely identified (v. 1); between the second and third Passover, the Feast of Tabernacles in October (vii. 2), and the Feast of the Dedication of the Temple in December (x. 22). The references being so definite, it is quite unlikely that a Passover feast has been passed over. We may therefore calculate that the public ministry of Jesus lasted, according to Jn., somewhat over two years (not, as is commonly said, three years).

The Synoptics, on the other hand, do not allow us to fix its duration. They know of no festival except that of the Passover on which Jesus died. The natural thing to do of course would be to supplement them on this point from Jn. But they tell us just as little of any one of the journeys which Jesus is supposed to have made at so many of these festivals. So that if we wished to bring them into agreement with Jn., the effort to do so would give rise to a complaint all the more serious, that they are silent about such important matters. If we are bent on discovering, by means of a calculation which is quite uncertain, how long the public ministry of Jesus is supposed to have lasted, we shall hardly find that it lasted more than one year; in fact, a few months would perhaps suffice to cover all that the Gospels relate.

2. SCENE OF JESUS' MINISTRY.

We have already had to touch upon another main point in which the other Gospels differ from Jn. It affects the scene of Jesus' ministry. According to the Synoptics, Jesus did not come to Jerusalem or to Judaea at all--the most southern of the three parts of the Jewish land lying between the east coast of the Mediterranean Sea and the Jordan, which flows from the north to the south into the Dead Sea--until a few days before his death. Previously he stayed uninterruptedly in Galilee, the northernmost of these three parts. The shores of the Lake of Gennesareth are here the chief scene of his ministry. On one occasion he journeyed outside of the land far to the north-west into the regions of Tyre and Sidon and back to the east shore of the Sea of Galilee (Mk. vii. 24, 31); afterwards he went once to the other side of the northern boundary of Galilee into the neighbourhood of Caesarea Philippi (Mk. viii. 27). His journey to Jerusalem led him eastward of Jordan through Peraea (Mk. x. 1); Samaria, which lay west of this, midway between Galilee and Judaea, which would have been his nearest way, was avoided because an old feud had made the Samaritans unfriendly in their attitude towards the Jews, especially when these were making pilgrimages to Jerusalem (Lk. ix. 52 f., Jn. iv. 9).

Nevertheless Lk., and he alone, does represent this journey as having been made through Samaria; in fact his account of it extends over nine whole chapters (ix. 51-xviii. 34). But he leads us to realise fully that he is not clear as to the facts of his story. Not very far from the end of it, for instance, he repeats (xvii. 11) that Jesus was on the way to Jerusalem, and adds that in the course of it he passed through the midst of Samaria and Galilee, whereas Galilee must have been left behind, if his purpose was to reach Jerusalem by way of Samaria. In xiii. 31 Jesus is warned against the snares of Herod Antipas, whose jurisdiction he had already avoided by leaving Galilee for Samaria. Further, on this journey Jesus is supposed on several occasions to have met Pharisees (xv. 2; xvii. 20), and is even said to have been invited to sit at meat with two of them (xi. 37; xiv. 1). But it is certain that no Pharisee could stay in Samaria, where he would come into daily contact with a people which did not observe the strict injunctions of the Jewish Law, and so would, of course, be continually defiled in such a way that no amount of washings and other observances would have availed to make him clean. Lk.'s story of Jesus journey through Samaria has therefore no claim to trustworthiness; it must be left entirely on one side.

In Jn. then the most important thing is this, that Jesus real and abiding dwelling-place during his ministry is Judaea and especially Jerusalem. To Galilee he came only on rare occasions and only for a short time: in ii. 1-12 to Cana at the marriage-feast and to Capernaum, where however he remained "not many days"; in iv. 43-v. 1 to Cana again, as regards which visit only the cure of the son of the royal official from Capernaum is signalised as a (special) event; finally in vi. 1 Jesus crosses the Lake of Galilee without its being said how he came there from Judaea; he feeds the five thousand, on the following night walks across the Lake, on the ensuing day teaches the people; and soon after the Feast of Tabernacles is again near at hand (vii. 2), for which he goes to Jerusalem without returning to Galilee. In the case of the last journey but one to Galilee we learn also where, according to Jn., Jesus original home really was, "Jesus himself testified that a prophet has no honour in his own country; when then he came to Galilee, the Galileans received him kindly" (iv. 44 f.). What is here meant by Jesus country? Judaea is intended, just as certainly as in the Synoptics his father's town Nazareth in Galilee is; for it was in Nazareth, as every one knows from Mk. (vi. 4), Mt., and Lk., that he uttered this saying (the Greek word patrís means both father's land and father's town). In i. 45 f.; vii. 41 f., 52, it is true, Jn., like the Synoptics, presupposes that Galilee, especially Nazareth, is Jesus native place, but in spite of this, iv. 44 f. implies the contrary. Moreover, vii. 42 suggests that Jn. may have believed that at least the birth of Jesus took place in Bethlehem, and so in Judaea.

As to the journeys northward from the Lake of Galilee, Jn. is entirely silent. Jesus comes to Peraea shortly before the last Passover according to Jn. also, but on this occasion not by the pilgrimage route from Galilee to Jerusalem, but from Jerusalem (x. 40), where he has stayed since the Feast of Tabernacles (vii. 2, 10), and so without break since October. But, besides this, according to Jn,, on the second excursion also which he makes from here to Galilee (not as in Lk. on the last journey to Jerusalem in the opposite direction), he comes to Samaria (iv. 1-4), and follows up the success which he has here with the woman at Jacob's Well and all the inhabitants of her town, by holding out the greatest expectations of extensive missionary work on the part of his disciples (iv. 35-38), though according to Mt. x. 5 he expressly forbids these same disciples to carry on mission work among the Samaritans. In short, a greater difference with regard to the scene of his ministry can hardly be imagined.

3. THE CLASSES OP PEOPLE AMONGST WHOM JESUS MOVED.

With whom then had Jesus to deal when he came forward to teach in public? In the Synoptics with the most different classes of people. Here we find crowds of people following him into the wilderness to listen to him for days together. The sick come and ask for healing, sometimes abashed like the woman with an issue of blood, who, with out being seen, hoped to be able to touch the hem of his garment (Mk. v. 25-34), sometimes, like blind Bartimaeus at Jericho, crying aloud (Mk. x. 46-48). A rich man desires to learn from the Master what he must do in order to attain everlasting life (Mk. x. 17); a scribe wishes to know which is the most important commandment in the Law of Moses (Mk. xii. 28); another would like to follow him, but does not reflect that Jesus has no place where he can lay his head (Mt. viii. 19 f.); others again desire to follow him, but would first bury their fathers (Mt. viii. 21 f.) or take solemn farewell of their friends (Lk. ix. 61 f.); yet another has a legacy dispute with his brother, and Jesus is to settle it (Lk. xii. 13 f.); the chief tax-gatherer Zacchaeus climbs up a mulberry-tree in order to see Jesus as he passes by (Lk. xix. 1-10). Another tax-gatherer, who may have been called Levi (so Mk. ii. 14 - Lk. v. 27) or Matthew (so Mt. ix. 9), at the beck of Jesus leaves his business to follow him, and at the meal which he prepares afterwards we find Jesus in the midst of the tax-gatherers and their whole company, which was regarded as sinful, but which he so much cultivated that it came to be said, he is "a glutton and a wine-bibber, an associate of publicans and sinners" (Mt. xi. 19). It was at Levi's meal that the Pharisees and scribes, with long fringes to their garments (Mt. xxiii. 5) in token of a singular piety, were present to find fault with him, just as they opposed him everywhere else, raising objection in the name of the Law of Moses to his disciples plucking ears of corn on the Sabbath or to his doing work on the Sabbath by healing a sick man (Mk. ii. 23-iii. 6), or to his declaring that the sins of the paralytic man were forgiven (Mk. ii. 1-12). And he on his part is never tired of pronouncing against that hypocrisy and affectation of holiness of theirs through which they allow themselves to be surprised at prayer in the street, that they may keep their piety well in evidence, and at the same time consume the houses of widows and declare it to be a work well pleasing to God to give to the Temple something which is needed for the support of one's own poor parents (Mk. vii. 11-13; Mt. vi. 5 and chap. xxiii.). In return they try to set snares for him and by captious questions to entice from him an utterance on the strength of which proceedings may be taken against him. And the Sadducees, the aristocratic priestly party, which gave itself up to the joys of life, but held firmly to its position of authority and was relentless in matters of the law, also associated themselves with these efforts (Mk. xii. 18-27).

Where is all this varied picture in Jn.? Only a few of its features confront us there. In Jn. also the Pharisees vigilantly enforce the command that the Sabbath shall not be profaned by any work (ix. 14-16). But what Jesus finds fault with in them, apart from this, is not their factitious holiness, but only their unwillingness to believe in him. In Jn. not only do the Scribes not appear, but--and this is far more important--the publicans and sinners, the poor and oppressed, are missing also. As the particular persons with whom Jesus had to do, apart from his disciples and the sick persons whom he healed, mention can be made only of his mother (at the marriage feast of Cana, ii. 1-11, and at the cross, xix. 25-27), Nicodemus (iii. 1-21; vii. 50-52; xix. 39-42), the woman of Samaria (iv. 7-30), and Martha and Mary (at the raising of their brother Lazarus, xi. 1-44, and at the anointing of Jesus, xii. 1-8).

For the rest, Jesus is confronted only by a single class of men, "the Jews." Over thirty times this expression recurs in the first eleven chapters. Of course in the Synoptics also they are all Jews with whom Jesus holds intercourse; but in them a distinction is actually made between Jews and Jews, which is not made here. Every thing remains indefinite. To the sick man who was healed at the Pool of Bethesda, "the Jews" say, "it is the Sabbath, and it is not lawful for thee to carry thy bed" (v. 10). After he has learned who healed him, he tells "the Jews," it was Jesus (v. 15). Was he not himself a Jew then? And was not Jesus also a Jew? The Gospel of Jn. is very liable to make us forget this. Jesus journeys to Jerusalem not for this and that feast, which since he was a child of his people was a festival for him also, but to "the feast of the Jews"; with the exception of the Feast of the Dedication of the Temple (x. 22) all the feasts mentioned in Jn. and referred to above (p. 9 f.) are described in this way. Jesus says to the Pharisees, and another time to "the Jews," "in your law it is written" (viii. 17; x. 34); for Jesus himself, then, this Law is not valid. We even read in vii. 11-13 that at Jerusalem "none spake openly about him for fear of the Jews." Here by the Jews cannot be meant the whole population, but only the authorities whose attitude was particularly hostile to Jesus. The strange expression indicates, however, that the same hostile feeling is imagined to prevail among the whole people.

4. COURSE OF JESUS' MINISTRY.

In accordance with this, as far as the course of Jesus' ministry is concerned it might now be expected to have a very speedy and a violent termination. In particular, it was the expulsion of the dealers from the fore-court of the Temple that, according to the account of the Synoptics, sealed Jesus fate. And, as a matter of fact, no officials could allow their sacred rights to be interfered with in this way without letting all authority slip out of their hands. But in Jn. the expulsion takes place at the beginning of Jesus' public ministry, and it happens with out bringing upon him any serious consequences. This is all the more remarkable since in this Gospel no difficulties seem to be felt at all when Jesus is represented as about to be taken prisoner without any clear legal grounds for the action. The High-priests and Pharisees only need to give their agents command to effect the capture (vii. 32). It is not effected, it is true. But why not? Their agents allow themselves to be withheld from obeying their instructions by the power of Jesus' words, and the authorities quietly abandon their object (vii. 45-49). We are told repeatedly that "they" (or "the Jews") sought to take him or to kill him (v. 18; vii. 1; viii. 37, 40; x. 31), but the result is always: "none laid hand upon him" (vii. 30), "he escaped from their hands" (x. 39), or when they wished to stone him, "he hid himself and escaped from the Temple place" (viii. 59). And the reason given is that "his hour was not yet come" (vii. 30; viii. 20).

Now certainly it must not be overlooked that in the Synoptics also (Mk. iii. 6) the Pharisees with the party of Herod took counsel together how they might destroy Jesus after his first cure of a sick man on a Sabbath. On the whole, however, events run their course here in a much more intelligible way. Jesus comes forward in Galilee and finds favour--even an enthusiastic welcome--among the people for a whole period. The intervention of the Pharisees is powerless to check this. When Jesus leaves Jewish territory on the north, he does so expressly in order to escape the pressure now becoming too great (Mk. vii. 24). Only in the end does there come a time when he finds himself called upon to go up to Jerusalem, and there, by means of a solemn entry into the city, to force a decision of the question whether people would see in him the Saviour (Mk, xi. 1-11). The decision follows within few days, and is hastened chiefly by the expulsion of the dealers from the fore-court of the Temple.

In the Fourth Gospel, on the other hand, although the circumstances urgently require an immediate settlement of the question, it is deferred again and again; and, finally the decision is caused by an event of which the Synoptics know nothing at all--by the raising of Lazarus. The greatest of all miracles leads the High Council, the highest authority among the Jewish people, to meet together and definitely contemplate Jesus' removal (xii. 47-53, 57). Thus the two accounts do not agree even to what really provided the occasion for the overthrow Jesus.

5. JESUS' WORKS OF WONDER.

As to the fact that Jesus worked miracles, it is true, they are all agreed. And it is only on the surface that the number, according to Jn.'s account, has to be thought of as somewhat limited. He, as a matter of fact, continually presupposes that it was large (ii. 23; iv. 45; vi. 2; vii. 31; xi. 47; xii. 37; xx. 30), and in xx. 31 expressly says that he has only included a selection of them in his book. And yet it is significant that among these that class of miracles is not found which not only, according to the Synoptics, was the most common, but also (according to the general agreement of modern historians and theologians of every school) least deserves to be doubted--we mean the cure of so-called possessed persons or demoniacs, that is to say, of the mentally sick, a cure which is effected by physicians fairly often even in our own times.

Next, it must certainly appear strange that the miracles reported in Jn. are often more marvellous in their character than those in the corresponding narratives of the Synoptics. Amongst the stories of cures in the Synoptics we do not hear of a man being healed by Jesus who had been ill for thirty-eight years; nor amongst the references to blind men, of sight being given to one who was born blind. The daughter of Jairus, according to Mk. v. 22-43, was raised very soon after her death; the young man at Nain, according to Lk. vii. 11-17, on the way to burial, which in the hot climate of Palestine took place on the very day of death, or, according to the story of Ananias and Sapphira in the Acts of the Apostles (v. 5 f., 10), immediately after death (cp. also Tobit viii. 10-16). To understand what a difference is implied when we are told that Lazarus was not resuscitated until the fourth day after his death, we must bear in mind the Jewish idea that the soul hovered about a dead body for three days after death and was ready to return to it. On the fourth day it finds the appearance of the dead person so completely altered that it forsakes it once and for all.

It would also be a great mistake to suppose that the description of the walking on the Lake of Galilee is more easy to accept in Jn.'s account (vi. 16-21) than in that of the Synoptics (Mk. vi. 45-52), because it is supposed to admit of a perfectly natural explanation. Thus stress is laid on the fact that the Greek words, Jesus walked "upon the sea," might also mean "by the sea," and it is assumed that the disciples with their boat, without noticing it, kept quite near the shore or had come near it again; Jesus passed close by the water's edge, and it was only the high waves that made it appear as if he walked upon the water. This conception is supposed to find further support in the concluding words (Jn. vi. 21), "they wished then to take him into the ship, and immediately the ship struck the land." On this view there is only one thing omitted, and that is the chief point we mean the four words which follow, "to which they steered." By this, as we are expressly told in vi. 11 is meant the opposite shore of the sea. The Evangelist, therefore, really emphasises the fact that Jesus walked across the whole sea and did not need to be taken into the boat, as in the Synoptics.

Yet another view is suggested by the changing of the water into wine at the marriage-feast at Cana (Jn. ii. 1-11). This miracle is one which Jesus performed not on a man but on an inanimate object, and hardly any one can say that it was prompted by heartfelt compassion for suffering humanity. The Evangelist also assigns to it a quite different meaning: "this was the first sign which Jesus did and whereby he announced his majesty." Not every work of wonder is in itself a "sign" of this kind. Any one of them of course may be such a "sign," if its purpose is to accredit the divine power of the worker; and many works of wonder must necessarily be regarded as "signs" in this sense, because no other purpose can be recognised in them.

Now the Synoptics also report certain works of wonder of this kind, for example the withering of the fig-tree after Jesus had cursed it (Mk. xi. 12-14, 20 f.), and we must certainly assume that other miracles of Jesus as well, works of wonder done from compassion, seemed to them to be "signs" quite as much as anything else. Nevertheless, the distinction still holds good that compassion as the ruling idea of the wonder-works of Jesus is in these as much in the foreground as it is in the background in Jn. The latter mentions not merely, as we have just noted, that the turning of the water into wine at Cana was the first miracle, but also says expressly that the healing of the son of the royal official of Capernaum was "the second sign which Jesus did in Galilee" (iv. 54); in fact he uses the word "sign" continually for Jesus' works of wonder, and in this Gospel Jesus emphasises the idea (v. 36; x. 25) that these "works," by which he means his works of wonder, are witnesses that he has been sent by God, and that though one refuses to believe his words, one must believe his "works" (x. 38; xiv. 11).

Now the view thus taken by Jn. is directly opposed to an utterance of Jesus preserved to us in the Synoptics. When the Pharisees wish to see a "sign" from him, he answers "there shall no sign be given unto this generation." So Mk. viii. 11-13. In Mt. (xii. 39; xvi. 4) and Lk. (xi. 29) he adds "except the sign of the prophet Jonah." It almost seems as if this addition were in full contradiction with Mk.'s account. But appearances are deceptive. That is to say, by the "sign of Jonah" is meant something which is really no sign at all--in fact the contrary of a sign. This unusual mode of expression is very effective. An illustration will make this clear at once. Suppose that a conqueror suddenly invades a country, that the inhabitants send ambassadors to him and ask for credentials to justify his raid, and that he answers, "no credentials shall be given to you but the credentials of my sword." And the idea in Jesus' words about the sign of Jonah is really similar, for he says in continuation, "the people of Nineveh shall rise up in judgment with this generation (with which I have to deal), and shall condemn it, for they repented at the preaching of Jonah, and behold a greater than Jonah is here "in my person (Mt. xii. 41). Here we are actually told in what the sign of Jonah consists: it is his preaching. And what Jesus has to offer--though in a more perfect form--is of course also preaching. He desires merely to preach, not to do "signs." Nor is this a principle which he sets before himself one day and ignores the next. The generation of the Pharisees was not unworthy one day and worthy the next to see a "sign" from him. Here then we have evidence of priceless value to show that Jesus declined on principle to do, not all works of wonder, but all such as might be supposed to serve the purpose of accrediting his exalted rank. And he must really have uttered these words, for none of all his recorders who believed that Jesus really did works of wonder with this intention would have invented them.

In order to emphasise fully the importance of such passages, we describe them as foundation-pillars of a really scientific Life of Jesus. That is to say, every historian in whatever field he may work, in a story which shows that the author worshipped his hero, follows the principle of regarding as true anything that runs counter to this worship, because it cannot be due to invention. Since we possess several Gospels, we are in a position to note, in addition, how one or more of them will sometimes remodel, sometimes remove altogether, passages of this nature because they were too offensive to one who worshipped Jesus. In their original form, therefore, such passages show us most certainly how Jesus really lived and thought, that he did so in a way which we--though we fully recognise in him something divine--must describe as truly human. Secondly, if it were not for such passages we could not be sure that we may, to some extent at least, rely upon the Gospels in which they are found, that is to say upon the first three. If they were entirely wanting in them it would be difficult to reply to the claim that the Gospels nowhere present to us anything but the figure of a saint delineated on a background of gold, and that we cannot know how Jesus really lived and worked, nor perhaps whether he even lived at all. The foundation-pillars on which, in addition to that mentioned above, we may lean in our effort to gain a correct idea of the wonder works of Jesus, will be discussed on p. 41, and in Chap. III., §§ 18 and 19; the rest which are important for other sides of Jesus character, on pp. 24 f., 26 f., 27 f., 29 and 43.

Naturally all that we find to be trustworthy in the Synoptics is by no means limited to these nine "foundation-pillars." It is one of the chief duties of a historian to show that the success which a great character has had in history can be understood from his words and works. But in the case of Jesus the success has been so great that even an inquirer who is quite sober in his attitude towards him must search out and accept as true everything that was calculated to establish his greatness and to make the worship which was offered to him by his contemporaries intelligible, provided that it is not in conflict with the picture of Jesus presented by the foundation- pillars, and does not for other reasons arouse in us doubts which are well founded.

Coming back to Jesus' words about the "sign of Jonah," after what has already been said about it, it may be gathered how lacking in intelligence the man must have been who inserted, between the saying about the sign of Jonah and that about the people of Nineveh, the sentence "for as Jonah was three days and three nights in the belly of the whale, so shall the Son of Man be three days and three nights in the heart of the earth." Moreover, this insertion is found only in Mt. xii. 40, not in Mt. xvi., nor in Lk. and Mk. What then is meant? The day will come when the Pharisees shall see the miracle of Jesus resurrection. And then we are told further in Mt. that "the people of Nineveh . . . repented at the preaching of Jonah." Did Jonah preach to them about his coming forth from the belly of the fish? And if he had done so, could it have made much impression upon them? A miracle one wishes to see with one's own eyes, not merely to hear about. But, besides this, we are told quite correctly, in agreement with the Old Testament book which deals with Jonah, what it was that he preached to the people of Nineveh: it was repentance. Thus the idea introduced, that Jesus told the Pharisees they would one day see the miracle of his resurrection, is not appropriate here.

Why do we spend so much time on this point which is not found at all in the Fourth Gospel? The reason is that in this too (ii. 18-22) Jesus is asked to show a "sign" (in proof that he has the right to drive the dealers from the fore-court of the Temple), and that he does not decline to do so as in the Synoptics, but points to his future resurrection, just as he does in the inappropriate insertion in Mt.; this event will prove his right to have driven the sellers--two years previously--from the Temple court.

As regards the miracle at Cana we have still to note the rôle played in it by Jesus mother. Although down to this time Jesus has never worked a miracle (Jn. ii. 11), his mother foresees that he will do one, and says to the servants, even after she has been rebuked by Jesus, "whatsoever he shall command you, that do." How entirely different is the presentation of Mary in Mk.! Here (iii. 21) Jesus' friends go out to seize him because they think him mentally distraught. Who these friends are we are very soon told in Mk. (iii. 31-35); his mother and his brethren come and send some one to summon him from the house; and only their intention to withdraw him from his active work and banish him to his parents house will explain his gruff answer, "Who is my mother and my brethren? Whosoever doeth the will of God, he is my brother and sister and mother." We may take it for granted that when Mk. tells us of this intention, and of the idea that Jesus was mentally distraught, he was relying upon unimpeachable information. This is clear when we look into Mt. and Lk. They do not say a word about these two things--and why, unless it was because they dare not believe anything of the kind?--and give only Jesus' gruff answer, without of course reflecting what an unfavourable light is thrown upon Jesus, if it was not provoked by conduct on the part of his mother and his brethren which was quite intolerable.

6. THE GENERAL PICTURE OF JESUS.

The conception which we have formed of Jesus as a worker of wonders will affect to an important extent the picture of him which is formed as a whole. Here again it will not be forgotten that the Synoptics agree with Jn. in sketching it with a grandeur which raises Jesus to a marked extent above the standard of what is human. Yet they report that he also, like others, was baptized by John. In the Fourth Gospel we look in vain for this information. Here we find only the later report of the Baptist, that lie saw the Holy Spirit coming down upon Jesus from heaven like a dove; and even this is supposed to have happened, not for the sake of Jesus, but only of the Baptist the purpose being that by this sign which God had already announced to him, he might be able to recognise in the person who stood before him the Son of God whom he did not already know (i. 32-34).

In Jn. also the fact recorded by the Synoptics (Mt. iv. 1-11), that Jesus was tempted by the devil, is entirely omitted. And to this Evangelist the report in Mk. (x. 17 f.) and Lk., that Jesus, when a rich man said to him, "Good master, what must I do to inherit eternal life?" answered, "Why callest thou me good? None is good but God alone" would have been equally unacceptable. And yet without doubt this answer came from Jesus lips. How little any of those worshippers who noted down the records in the Gospels could have invented it is shown by Mt. In Mt. (xix. 16 f.) the rich man says, "Master, what good thing must I do in order to have eternal life?" And Jesus answers, "Why askest thou me concerning what is good? One is the good." How in this passage does Jesus come to add the last four words? Should he not, since he was questioned about the good, have continued, "one thing is the good"? And this would have been the only appropriate reply, not only in view of what precedes, but also on account of what follows, for Jesus says later, "but if thou wilt enter into life, keep the commandments." Thus it is in the keeping of the commandments, Jesus thinks, that that good thing consists about which he was asked. How does Mt. get the words, "one is the good"? Simply by having before him, when he wrote, the language of Mk. Here we have a practical example of the way in which Mt. deliberately tried so to change this language at the beginning as to make it inoffensive, while at the end, in spite of his purpose, he left unchanged a few words of it which reveal to us what has happened and how it arose. But by removing in this way the words of Jesus to the effect that he did not deserve to be called good, Mt. has only anticipated the Fourth Gospel in which Jesus exclaims triumphantly (viii. 46), "Which of you convicteth me of sin? "

In the Synoptics (Mk. xiv. 32-39) we are told that in the Garden of Gethsemane Jesus prayed insistently that the cup of death might pass from him. In Jn. we seek for this information in vain. The words about the cup, familiar to us from the Synoptics, are used by Jesus in Jn. also, but in the contrary sense, "the cup which the Father hath given me, shall I not drink it?" (xviii. 11). We find in a much earlier passage (xii. 27) the only thing that can be compared with the deep emotion of Jesus in Gethsemane. Several days before his death Jesus says here, "Now is my soul troubled, and what shall I say? "But no more unsuitable continuation could be imagined than the following words when they are mistranslated, "Father, deliver me from this hour." How can the Jesus of the Fourth Gospel think of asking the Father in heaven to deliver him from death? He actually gives up his life of his own accord (x. 17 f.). The sentence can therefore only be meant as a question: "What ought I to say? Ought I to say, Father, deliver me from this hour?'" This alone makes the following words also appropriate, "but for this cause came I unto this hour"; therefore I say, "Father, glorify thy name," by letting me go to my death.[2]

Mk. (xv. 34) and Mt. at any rate have the saying of Jesus from the cross, "My God, my God, why hast thou forsaken me?" In Jn., as well as in Lk., we fail to find it. And yet we may be quite certain that it was no more invented than the saying about the sign of Jonah. An indication of weakness in the Crucified Lord might be found in the saying in Jn. xix. 28, "I thirst," which, in turn, is not found in the Synoptics. But the author has been careful at the outset to exclude this interpretation. He says expressly that Jesus spoke the word in order that a prophecy of the Old Testament (Ps. xxii. 16) might be fulfilled; we are not therefore meant to suppose that Jesus was really thirsty.

Furthermore, we read frequently in the Synoptics that Jesus prayed to his heavenly Father, and that he sought solitude for this purpose (e.g., Mk. i. 35). How Jn. thinks of Jesus as praying is clear when he is represented as standing before the open sepulchre of Lazarus (xi. 41 f.) and saying, "Father, I thank thee that thou heardest me. And I know that thou hearest me always; but because of the multitude which standeth around I said it, that they may believe that thou didst send me." From this it appears that Jesus did not need to pray for his own sake, but only for that of the people; and this he even explains to God in a prayer. Here that power of his to do wonders, with which we started, is first revealed in its fullest light.

To this may now be added the continual examples of his omniscience. Nathanael, who has only just come to him, Jesus has already seen under the fig-tree before Philip called him to Jesus (i. 48). He did not trust himself to those who believed on him at the first Passover feast in Jerusalem, because he knew them all (ii. 24 f.). He was able to tell the woman of Samaria, that she had had five husbands, and that he whom she now had was not her husband, and she was obliged to admit on the strength of this that Jesus was a prophet (iv. 16-19). As regards Lazarus he received a message merely to the effect that he was sick. But Jesus knew that in the meantime he had died (xi. 3 f. 11-14; see p. 32). He knew "from the beginning" that Judas Iscariot would betray him (vi. 64; xiii. 18), In the Synoptics, on the other hand, we find him expressly declaring that (Mk. xiii. 32) "of that day," that is to say, the day on which he would come down from heaven, in order to set up the Kingdom of God upon earth, "or of that hour knoweth no one, not even the angels in heaven, neither the Son, but the Father"--another of the sayings which, we may be sure, none of his worshippers has invented. Lk. omits it altogether; Mt. (according to what is probably the original text) omits at least the all-important words "neither the Son."

We may add further the continual examples of that inviolability of his, which we have already referred to (above, p. 17): they wished to seize him, but he suffered no harm. It will have become clear in the meantime that the expression which occurs here, "he hid himself" (viii. 59; also xii. 36), certainly cannot mean that Jesus concealed himself, but only--as his dignity would require--that he made himself invisible in a miraculous way, because "his hour had not yet come."

When, however, his hour came, he gave himself up of his own accord. Once more we read that the soldiers could do him no harm; at his words. "It is I" whom ye seek, they go back and fall to the ground (500, if not 1000, Roman soldiers). Judas, since it was dark, according to the Synoptics (Mk. xiv 44 f.) requires to point him out first by kissing his hand; in Jn. he does not need to do so, he stands idly by (xviii. 3-6). Jesus of his own accord, by dipping a morsel in the sop and giving it to Judas at the Last Supper, made the devil enter into him, and himself bade him hasten his evil deed (xiii. 26 f.) and of this again the Synoptics know nothing.

7. GENUINE HUMAN CHARACTERISTICS IN JESUS?

But, this being so, does the description of Jesus in the Fourth Gospel embody no genuinely human characteristics? It is significant that even those who still place this Gospel on a higher level than the other three would rather the picture of Jesus were not so like a God as it is in the description we have just given, following faithfully the real idea of the author But of all that they can point to, the only thing which is at all worthy of consideration is found in the words (xi. 35), "Jesus wept"--the occasion being when he came near to the grave of Lazarus. And the idea that we have here an instance of real human emotion on the part of Jesus seems, further, to be confirmed expressly by the following words: "The Jews therefore said, Behold how he loved him.'" But this of itself is necessarily startling. We shall very soon (p. 44 f.) have to explain that what the Jews say in reply to a declaration by Jesus is in the Fourth Gospel regularly based upon a misunderstanding. But, further, the author has taken care to make it clear to every one who is at pains to understand him that the words of the Jews are shown by the context of the passage itself to be a misunderstanding. Before this it has been said (xi. 33): "When Jesus therefore saw Mary weeping, and the Jews also weeping which came with her, he groaned in the spirit and was troubled." After the words of the Jews, "Behold, how he loved him," we are told further, "But some of them said, Could not this man, which opened the eyes of him that was blind, have caused that this man also should not die?'" Jesus, again groaning in his spirit, now goes to the grave. Why did he groan in this way? Now this second time we are clearly told, it was because the Jews who are here speaking did not think that his power to raise Lazarus was to be regarded as something which he possessed quite as a matter of course. But why should he have groaned the first time? Surely because of something of the same nature, that is to say, simply because Mary and the Jews wept instead of confidently expecting that the dead man would be raised by Jesus. And when we are told, in the interval, that he wept, it should not really be so difficult to see that his tears were not on account of the loss of his friend and the mourning of Lazarus' kinsfolk--he knew well enough that at the next moment both would be obliterated by the raising of Lazarus--but simply because they did not believe in his power to work miracles.

Or if this cannot really be seen here, can it not be recognised even at the beginning of the narrative? If we were to read it aloud simply as far as the words in xi. 5 f., "Now Jesus loved Martha and her sister, and Lazarus. When therefore he heard that he was sick," certainly every listener would expect us to proceed, "then he went to him immediately." Instead of this we actually find the words, "he abode at that time two days in the place where he was." Why? Unless we are willing to believe that he feared the snares of the Jews, against which his disciples warn him in xi. 8 two days later--he himself refusing to take warning--we can only say that this delay was to all appearances due to an indifference or inhumanity which is superior to all genuinely human feeling. But it would be quite unfair to make his conduct a subject of moral criticism. The author of the Gospel has taken care to show that we may not, as a matter of fact, expect to find any genuinely human feeling in the Jesus of his story. After two days have passed, Jesus says to his disciples openly (xi. 14 f.): "Lazarus is dead; and I am glad for your sakes that I was not there, to the intent ye may believe." In what? This we have been told already, in xi. 4, where Jesus receives news of the illness of Lazarus: "This sickness is not unto death, but for the glory of God, that the Son of God may be glorified thereby."

The words at the beginning of this sentence mean, not that this sickness will not cause the death of Lazarus, but that it will not lead to his remaining dead, for, as the concluding words show, Jesus knew beforehand that he would raise Lazarus, and that the miracle would serve for his own glorification. And he could only effect this and exceed all other miracles if he allowed the fourth day to come before he arrived at the sepulchre, since only then could any return to life be considered out of the question (see p. 19). Here then we have the real reason why he delayed his journey for two days.

In this case we can prove something more. Since the journey to Bethany takes at most two days, and Jesus did not arrive there until the fourth day after Lazarus' death, Lazarus was already dead by the time the messengers reached Jesus, and the Fourth Gospel presupposes that Jesus already knew this, by means of course of that omni science with which it supposes him to be endowed. The sorrow of the sisters, their longing for a word of comfort, their anxious waiting for one who might have arrived long ago--all this is nothing to him; he is only concerned about the miracle and his own glorification. Here we can see whether the Jesus of the Fourth Gospel has any human characteristics.

8. DEVELOPMENT OF JESUS IN THE COURSE OF HIS WORK.

In the character of Jesus as described by the Synoptics we are allowed to see further that he developed both in thought and action. It would of course be a very great mistake to suppose that they themselves were conscious of any such development or believed in it. But they at any rate make such statements as enable us, when we carefully examine them, to discover this truth. It is at a relatively late date that Jesus in these Gospels is recognised by his disciples to be the ardently hoped-for deliverer of his people, the God-sent inaugurator of the kingdom of God, the Saviour, to use a popular term, or, as the Jewish name "Messiah" and the Greek name "Christus" mean, the "Anointed" of God. They do not report it, that is to say until the public ministry of Jesus had continued for a fairly long time, not until after he had found occasion to withdraw for the second time beyond the northern boundary of Galilee (Mk. viii. 27-30). The confession which Peter now made in Caesarea Philippi, in the name of the other disciples as well, was, according to the Synoptics, one of the most important turning-points. According to Jn., Peter made the corresponding pronouncement (vi. 66-69), not on foreign territory, but at Capernaum (Jn. knowing nothing of the journey farther north); but--and this is the chief point--it is not represented as a new discovery and announcement and as made for the first time. In truth, it cannot be such, for in this Gospel John the Baptist already knows, when he sees Jesus approaching him for the first time, that he is the Lamb of God which taketh away the sins of the world, and that he has existed before him (i. 29 f.) And Andrew, after he has been a day with Jesus, and even before Jesus' public appearance, is able to say to his brother Peter, "we have found the Messiah" (i. 38-41).

Next, in the Synoptics we find Jesus saying at one time that he has not come to destroy the Law of Moses, but only to fill it with its true import, and so to deepen it (Mt. v. 17) in a manner which is more precisely exemplified in Mt. v. 21 f. 27 f.; and at another time making such statements as, "the Sabbath was made for man, and not man for the Sabbath" (Mk. ii. 27), or "whatsoever from without goeth into the man, it cannot defile him, but only evil thoughts which proceed out of the heart" (Mk. vii. 18-23). Such declarations as these brush aside the whole Law, if we think of the literal meaning of its particular precepts. There is hardly any other way of reconciling the two classes of utterance but to suppose that Jesus expressed himself in the one way at an earlier period, and in the other at a later date.

Or when we read that Jesus went into foreign territory that he might remain unrecognised, and that at first he roughly repulsed the Phoenician woman who cried after him, beseeching him to heal her sick daughter, but after wards paid attention to her (Mk. vii. 24; Mt. xv. 21-28), certainly the natural explanation is that at first he seriously meant what he said to her: that it would be wrong to take the bread--that is to say, the power to heal, with which he was endowed--from the children (of the chosen people) and to give it to the dogs, that is to say, to the Gentiles, to whom she also belonged. It was only the affecting and very appropriate retort of the anxious mother, "even the dogs under the table eat of the children's crumbs," that could convert him, if this version is correct, and so prepare him to alter all his ideas about the extension of his lifework to the Gentiles.

Jn. does not give us the slightest clue to any such changes; Jesus in this Gospel suffers no alteration; he is the same from beginning to end.

9. FORM OF JESUS DISCOURSES.

The same contrast is seen again in a particularly clear way in Jesus' discourses. Here indeed the difference, as compared with the Synoptics, is perhaps most clearly marked. It is apparent even in the form. In the first three Gospels we have short, pithy utterances: "Blessed are the pure in heart, for they shall see God"; "ye have heard that it was said to those of old . . . but I say unto you . . ."; "they that are whole need not a physician, but they that are sick"; "what shall it profit a man if he gain the whole world and suffer loss of his own life" (Mt. v. 8, 21 f.; Mk. ii. 17; viii. 36). We might go on quoting utterances of this kind almost without end. Even where the discourses are longer, as in the Sermon on the Mount, or on the occasion when he sent forth the disciples, or in his address to the Pharisees (Mt. v.- vii., x., xxiii.), we can easily see that they are really compilations of such pithy utterances as these, each of which has a meaning and force of its own. In Jn. no more than a few of these utterances reappear.

Everywhere else in this Gospel we find long spun-out discourses about certain thoughts, which, moreover, are repeated on the most varied occasions. In order to gain some idea of their style, read for instance Jn. iii. 11-21; v. 19-47; viii. 12-59; or vi. 26-58.

Jesus parables are special gems in his discourses. We never cease to be charmed by their vividness, the freshness of their colouring, and their appropriate application to the religious and moral problems of life, and we feel that they really must have been the best means of bringing eternal truths home to simple people in whom dwells half unconsciously so deep a desire for them. The Fourth Gospel does not contain a single parable. The only passage that approaches the parabolic form is that in which Jesus compares himself to a vine and his disciples to the branches (xv. 1-8); but this is only a figurative discourse, not a story in which some action is represented as going on before our eyes, such as that of the sower scattering seed or the shepherd going in search of his lost sheep. Elsewhere we have in Jn., besides this, only the instances in which Jesus calls himself the good shepherd and the door of the sheepfold (x. 11-16; x. 1-10). The first is as beautiful as the second is peculiar. Who can think of Jesus as the door? The thought is employed here for the purpose of distinguishing two classes of teacher: the shepherds who come to their sheep by entering the door, and robbers who climb in by another way. But how Jesus can here represent the door cannot be made clear, and much less when he is immediately afterwards compared (x. 11-16), not to the door, but to the good shepherd the good shepherd, by whom we have just been led to think (x. 2-5) some one else was intended.

10. SUBJECT OF JESUS' DISCOURSES.

And with what do the discourses of Jesus deal? In the Synoptics almost exclusively with the question, What must one do to gain admittance into the Kingdom of God? And the answer to the question is well-nigh exhausted when it is summed up in the words, "Be pure in heart, love God and your neighbour, do God's will" (Mt. v. 8; xxii. 37-39; vii. 21). According to the circumstances, and the persons to whom it was given, it took on different occasions the most varied forms; but the point was always that what is required is moral conduct based on the fear of God. This is so, even where Jesus speaks of his own person and says that one must follow him, one must listen to him (for instance, in Mt. x. 37-40). He does not say this for his own sake, but on account of those whom he wishes, by speaking thus, to lead into the right path, which of course no one knew so well as he. Words which go beyond this and require people to recognise his exalted nature, such as, "every one who shall confess me before men, him will I also confess before my Father which is in heaven" (Mt. x. 32 f.) play a quite subordinate part. Jesus speaks about himself very seldom.

He does so all the more frequently in the Fourth Gospel. Here his person and its divine nature is almost the only subject of his discourses. Jesus' words to the sick man at Bethesda after his cure, "Sin no more, lest a worse thing befall thee" (v. 14) are indeed spoken for the sufferer's sake; but the whole discourse which follows down to the end of the chapter serves to elaborate the thought, that Jesus has been sent by God and that God through his miracles, as well as through the prophecies found in the Old Testament, bears witness to Jesus as His son. It is true that we find again in this chapter something which is said on account of Jesus' hearers, "He that heareth my word, and believeth him that sent me, hath eternal life" (v. 24); but this word of Jesus to which they are to listen, according to the immediately preceding verse amounts to this, that all ought to honour the Son as they honour the Father in heaven. The man born blind is healed, but no word is said to him that might be helpful for the nurture of his soul--his only gain is this, that he learns step by step who it was that healed him; and this again, to say the least, subserves the purpose of Jesus glorification of himself. At the very beginning of the cure (ix. 5), Jesus calls himself the Light of the World. This thought, to which he has already given expression in viii. 12, is amplified throughout chapter viii., and here the discourse frequently harks back to what we have mentioned from chapter v., the idea that God bears witness to Jesus as His son. In chapter vi. (26-58), it is true that it is in the interest of Jesus' hearers when we are told that they are to receive the true bread of life, but the important point on which the whole discourse turns is this, that Jesus himself is this bread of life.

And what are known as the Farewell-discourses of Jesus (chaps. xiii.-xvii.) are not at bottom different in character. They deal with the idea that, to help the followers of Jesus after his death, the Holy Spirit will come upon them, and guide them to the whole truth (xiv. 26; xvi. 13); but at least of equal importance is the other point, that it is not only God (so xiv, 16 f.), but also Jesus himself, who will send this Holy Spirit (xv. 26; xvi. 7), and even that he himself, regarded from another point of view, is this Holy Spirit (xiv. 18, identical with xiv. 17; also xiv. 28). Moreover, these chapters are full of sayings which expressly serve the purpose of Jesus own glorification: "he that hath seen me hath seen the Father" (xiv. 9, exactly as in xii. 45); "all things whatsoever the Father hath are mine" (xvi. 15); "I came out from the Father, and am come into the world" (xvi. 28). It may be nothing more than external corroboration of this, but it is significant all the same, that in the discourses of Jesus in Jn. the word "my" occurs much more than twice as often as in Mt., and the word "I" more than six times as often.

There is only one narrative in the Fourth Gospel in which the utterances of Jesus do not serve the purpose of his own glorification, but are spoken entirely for the sake of the persons with whom he is dealing; this is the story of the woman who was taken in adultery and brought to Jesus (vii. 53-viii. 11). "He that is without sin among you, let him first cast a stone at her"; and after her accusers have slunk away one after another, "Neither do I condemn thee; go thy way, from henceforth sin no more." These utterances read, in fact, as if Mk., Mt., or Lk. lay open before us. But, apart from this, there is hardly a scholar who does not agree that this narrative was not found originally in the Gospel of Jn. It is missing in copies which were made as late as in the fourth century or still later, and many particular words are found in it for which elsewhere Jn. regularly uses quite different terms.

11. DEMANDS MADE BY JESUS IN His DISCOURSES.

What demands does Jesus make of his hearers in those discourses which were really penned by the Fourth Evangelist? These can be expressed in a few words. "Believe in my person and its divine character." The man who was born blind, after he has been healed, gradually arrives at the conviction that he who has healed him must be a God fearing man, one who does God's will; he must be "from God," otherwise God would never have given him power to make a blind man see (ix. 31-33). But this alone is not sufficient. Jesus asks him afterwards: "Dost thou believe in the Son of Man?" And when he replies, "And who is he, Lord, that I may believe in him?" Jesus says, "He that speaketh with thee is he." And not until now is that point reached which was bound to be reached. The man exclaims, "Lord, I believe it," and offers worship to Jesus (ix. 38). On the other hand, the only reason for the enmity existing between Jesus and his many opponents is that they have no faith in him. They reproach him for ascribing to himself a rank which he does not possess, that is to say, for making himself equal to God by calling Him his Father in the sense that he came from Him as a man comes from his human father (v. 18); and he, on his side, reproaches them for having an evil will and refusing to recognise his divine origin (v. 40; viii. 45 f.).

In the Synoptics also Jesus requires faith. He says to Jairus on their way to his daughter, whose death has just been announced to him, "Fear not, only believe" (Mk. v. 36). But the faith referred to here and nearly everywhere else in these Gospels relates only to Jesus power of doing a saving act which will result in some one being restored to health. We have an example of this when it is said so often at the conclusion of a story of healing: "Thy faith hath saved thee" (Mk, v. 34, &c.). This is something essentially different from the belief in Jn., that Jesus has come down from heaven to earth. In the Synoptics we might translate the word more appropriately "trust" instead of "faith," whereas in the Fourth Gospel it is clear that this would be quite unsuitable. Moreover, according to the accounts in the Synoptics, Jesus hardly ever needs to ask for this trust in the way that he is continually obliged to in Jn.; it is offered to him spontaneously.

We have in fact unimpeachable evidence to show that when it was not cherished spontaneously, he never thought of asking people for it. When he came forward publicly in his native town, Nazareth, people scorned him because they knew whose son and brother he was, and he had to experience the truth that a prophet has no honour in his own country. Now we are further told in Mk. (vi. 5 f.): "And he could there do no mighty work, save that he laid his hands upon a few sick folk and healed them. And he marvelled because of their unbelief." He could not! Here again we have a report like that about the sign of Jonah (see p. 21 f.). We may be quite sure that it would not have found a place in our Gospels, if it had not been made by one who had himself observed the fact, and been handed on without alteration. How unacceptable it must have been to those later chroniclers who were all, Mk. not excepted, convinced of the power of Jesus to work miracles, is shown by Mt., in which it reads thus (xiii. 58): "And he did not many mighty works there because of their unbelief."

In the Synoptics, in yet another sense Jesus asks for faith, even if the word "faith" does not occur. According to our way of expressing it, it is faith that he asks for when he says, for instance, "Follow me, and I will make you fishers of men" (Mk. i. 17), or "Ye have heard that it was said to them of old . . . but I say to you . . ." (Mt. v. 21 f.). But again the faith here meant is not, as in Jn., faith in the fact of Jesus descent from heaven, but simply confidence in his knowledge of the right way that leads to salvation.

Quite different from the Synoptics then is the method of Jn. when he makes the person of Jesus and its divine origin the central feature in Jesus' discourses. The language agrees fairly well with theirs when the Fourth Gospel also represents Jesus as requiring people to hear his words and to keep them (viii. 31, 51; cp. Mt. vii. 24; xxiv. 35); but what he asks of people in these words of his is not, as in the Synoptics, moral conduct, but acceptance as true of his assurance that he has come from heaven. This acceptance is even described as "the work "required by God (vi. 29). It is not a question of the kingdom of God and the way to reach it, but of Jesus person and the acknowledgment of his exalted nature. On one point certainly all the Gospels agree--in saying that love is the highest commandment (Mk. xii. 30 f.; Jn. xiii. 34 f.). The difference, however, is this, that, according to Jn., if love is not accompanied by this faith in the heavenly origin of Jesus, it can be of no value and can never be the path by which entrance is made into the kingdom of God. That is made quite clear by the saying of Jesus in Jn. (iii.

18): "He that believeth on him (the son of God) is not judged; he that believeth not hath been judged already, because he hath not believed on the name of the only begotten Son of God."

In Jn. therefore Jesus knows of nothing more important than his own person; do people believe in its divine origin or not?--the answer to this question decides whether men are to be saved or lost for time and eternity. In the Synoptics he knows of something higher. He says in Mt. xii. 31 f.: "All sins and blasphemy will be forgiven to men, but blasphemy against the Spirit will not be for given. And whosoever shall speak a word against the Son of man, it shall be forgiven him; but whosoever shall speak against the Holy Spirit, it shall not be forgiven him, neither in this world, nor in that which is to come." Thus he regards his own person as subordinate to the Holy Spirit, or in other words to the sacred cause which he represents. And he must really have said this; for no one would have invented it. Indeed Mk., who in this passage (iii. 28 f.) by no means preserves the original language, has obviously changed it with a definite purpose. He has retained the phrase "Son of man," but no longer uses it in such a way as to mean that the person of Jesus suffers the blasphemy; he applies it, in the plural, to the persons who utter it: "All their sins shall be forgiven unto the sons of men, and their blasphemies wherewith soever they shall blaspheme; but whosoever shall blaspheme against the Holy Spirit hath never forgiveness."

12. MISUNDERSTANDINGS AS REGARDS JESUS' DISCOURSES.

The large measure of uniformity in the discourses of Jesus in the Fourth Gospel means that these in themselves very soon reach their end. Nevertheless, some misunderstanding, on the part of his hearers, gives Jesus remarkably frequent occasion to prolong them. Sometimes indeed it is not surprising that his hearers do not understand him for example, when he tells them that he is the bread come down from heaven (vi. 41 f.), that he will give them his flesh to eat (vi. 52), that Abraham has already seen him (viii. 56 f.), etc.

In other passages, however, we are obliged to ask, on the contrary, whether the intelligence of his hearers could really have been so feeble. Nicodemus--to give a single instance--is said to have been a teacher in Israel (iii. 10), and yet he does not understand Jesus when he says, "whosoever is not born from above, cannot see the kingdom of God." He asks in astonishment, "How can a man be born when he is old? Can he enter a second time into his mother's womb and be born?" (iii. 3 f.).

But perhaps we have not been fair to him. We have rendered the words of Jesus according to their real sense: from above, that is to say from God, must he be born, by God must he be destined and endowed, who is to have admittance into the kingdom of God. But the words admit of another translation: "If any one is not born anew, he cannot see the kingdom of God." This is evidently the meaning which Nicodemus attaches to the words when he puts his counter-question, and this, at least externally, is not so senseless. Such ambiguity in Jesus language is no accident; it occurs again on very many occasions. When, as we have just mentioned, Jesus promises to give bread or meat to his hearers, on first thoughts and until we have realised that there is a deeper meaning in the words, we cannot help thinking that he really means ordinary food. It is the same with the water, which, as he sits by a well, Jesus promises to give the woman of Samaria, and of which he says that, after tasting it, she will never thirst again (iv. 13-15); and other instances occur frequently (e.g., iv. 31-34; vii. 33-36; viii. 31-33; xi. 11-14; xii. 32-34). We see that it is a peculiarity of these discourses, that in them Jesus chooses an expression with more meanings than one, and thus intentionally provokes misunderstanding, in order that he may afterwards explain the matter more precisely.

But at the same time another purpose is served. How can Philip, who has spent two years with Jesus, desire him to show him the heavenly Father (xiv. 8 f .)? This seems inconceivable even if he did not understand the words spoken by Jesus immediately before: "If ye had known me, ye would have known my father also; from henceforth ye know him, and have seen him." But we ourselves are perhaps surprised at the further statement which Jesus makes in reply to Philip's request, "Have I been so long time with you, and dost thou not know me, Philip? He that hath seen me hath seen the Father." We ourselves might still have thought perhaps that the recognition of the Father, as Philip may be supposed to have reached it from his acquaintance with Jesus, consisted in gaining a true idea of God's attributes, of His power, His wisdom, His goodness. Instead of this, however, Jesus thinks that we ought not to conceive of God here as a Being who has an existence independent of and separate from other beings, but ought to see Him presented to our objective vision in the person of Jesus himself. This in fact goes beyond all that we are accustomed to think we know about God. And so Philip's misunderstanding--as well as many others in Jn.--serves the further purpose of revealing in a particularly clear manner, on the one hand the lack of intelligence on the part of Jesus' hearers and even of his disciples, and on the other the infinite depth and unsuspected novelty of Jesus interpretations.

That the lack of intelligence in Jesus' hearers and even in his disciples was not slight, is indicated often enough by the Synoptics also. On the other hand, their books do not suggest that Jesus teaching contained such unfathomable secrets, nor are they aware that he was so continually misunderstood, or that he himself provoked these misunderstandings by using expressions with more meanings than one.

Footnote:

2. Marks of interrogation and other marks of inter-punctuation are not found in our ancient copies of the Bible. We must therefore supply them as best suits the sense.

CHAPTER II - ATTEMPTS TO RECONCILE THE FIRST THREE GOSPELS WITH THE FOURTH.

WE might have shown many other differences between the Synoptics and Jn. But it will be better to notice them at a later stage. We shall therefore pause here to deal with a question which must have occurred to many of our readers long before this: Are the accounts in the four Gospels really so fundamentally different? Is there no way of reconciling them?

1. EARLIER ATTEMPTS TO RECONCILE THEM COMPLETELY.

This question was quite urgent in the days when people felt obliged to cherish the belief that every letter in Holy Scripture was dictated by the Holy Spirit. In those days it had to be answered in the affirmative at any cost. And, as a matter of fact, the cost was not light--it did not involve merely effort and ingenuity, but meant giving up what seems obvious when the Bible is understood in a natural and unsophisticated way. And yet the attempt to establish complete harmony between the four Gospels (or, as was thought, simply the art of exhibiting this harmony), the nature of which suggested the name "Harmonics," was for many centuries one of the chief pursuits of theological science.

Strictly speaking, there are only two courses open to us, If one and the same event seems to be reported in more Gospels than one, but in a more or less different way, we must either show that the difference in the statement is only apparent, or we must say that each account treats of a distinct event. The more seriously we regard the language, the more frequently will the second course be the one we shall have to take. Strict Harmonics, too, with quite special frequency arrives at this result by starting with the presupposition that each Evangelist not only tells us a story correct in every word, but also gives each particular event and utterance in the life of Jesus in its right order, though--and this could not be denied under any circumstances--he omits many things which are preserved in the other Gospels.

Thus, for example, it was necessary to show in each of the first three Gospels at what point each of those journeys of Jesus to a feast reported only in Jn. could be fitted in. In Jesus' walking on the sea, Jn. (vi. 16-21), we are told, has not in mind the same event as the Synoptists have, for in the Synoptics Jesus is taken into the boat in the middle of the Lake (Mk. vi. 51), but in Jn. is not (see above, p. 19 f .). Again, the Feeding of the Five Thousand reported by Jn. (vi. 1-13) must be a different event from the Feeding spoken of by the Synoptics (Mk. vi. 35-44) for in all the Gospels we are told that such a feeding took place on the day preceding the night on which Jesus walked on the sea (with the exception of Lk. who does not report the walking on the sea). But how? It is not permissible even to regard the Feeding reported in all three Synoptics as one and the same event; for in Mt. (xiv. 21) those who are fed are more numerous--besides the 5000 men there are women and children the number of whom is not given. Consequently, there are three Feedings instead of one, in which the number 5000 figures: one in Mk. = Lk., another in Mt., a third in Jn. On each occasion there are only five loaves and two fishes ^ on each occasion twelve baskets full of fragments are gathered up; each event is followed by a night-journey across the sea; yet each Evangelist relates only one of these three events, and Mk. and Mt., though each knows of another Feeding, do not report more than one of these three; but the two between them tell of a fourth and a fifth--one according to Mk. (viii. 1-9) in which 4000 men, and another according to Mt. (xv. 32-38) in which 4000 men besides an indefinite number of women and children, were satisfied; but on both occasions this happens after the people have wandered about with Jesus for three days, on both occasions there are seven loaves and a few fishes, and on both occasions seven baskets full of fragments are gathered up afterwards.

But enough! The perseverance with which people have pursued all these suggestions--which from the outset are such as we cannot accept--to their utmost limit, and have put faith in them out of respect for the Holy Spirit, who is supposed to have inspired every letter of the Bible, certainly deserves to be fully recognised. Only one question is forbidden. How often may Jesus be supposed to have been born, baptized, crucified, and raised from the dead?

2. MODERN ATTEMPTS TO RECONCILE THEM APPROXIMATELY.

Present-day defenders of the trustworthiness of all the four Gospels are far more modest in the claims which they make. They quietly assume that one and the same event is meant, even where the accounts differ from one another rather widely; only they would rather not concede too much, and so they try as far as possible to represent the differences as being only slight. Naturally it is right for us always to test whether these are really as great as they seem at first sight to be. Where, however, this attempt is vain unless we seriously misinterpret the language, it is not only unfair, but is also nothing better than illogical. For if we are obliged to admit, and actually do admit, that there are many contradictions in the Bible, there is no point in insisting in the case of a limited number of these, that they are not really contradictions. If we admit--since Jesus was taken captive only on one occasion--that according to the Synoptics Judas betrayed him by a kiss, and according to Jn. did not betray him in this way (xviii. 4-6), what is the use, when we turn to the expulsion of the dealers from the fore-court of the Temple, of denying that either the Synoptists or Jn. must have made a mistake, and of preferring to suppose that there were two such acts, one at the beginning of his ministry (Jn. ii. 13-22), the other at the end of it (Mk. xi. 15-18)? If this were so, why did Jesus omit to drive the dealers and money-changers from the temple court on his other visits to Jerusalem as well? Are we to suppose that they were not stationed there on these occasions? And why on the first occasion did he escape scot free, whereas on the second he suffered death in consequence?

3. USE OF THE SYNOPTICS BY JN.

We may set aside such palpably impossible attempts to deny that there are contradictions between the Synoptics and Jn., and give attention to such as are really worth discussing. But before we do this, it should be said that it is almost universally agreed that the author of the Fourth Gospel had the other three before him when he wrote.

To prove this we are not of course at liberty to cite at our pleasure all kinds of things in which Jn. agrees with them, for these he might himself have noted as an eye witness. We must specify passages which he would not certainly have written, if he had not derived them from the Synoptics. Thus, for example, it is very remarkable that Jesus ascends the mountain before the Feeding of the Five Thousand (Jn. vi. 3) and ascends the mountain after it (vi. 15), though we have not been told in the meantime that he came down, or been given any clue that would lead us to conjecture that he did so. The matter admits of a simple explanation: when the author was about to relate the beginning of the Feeding, he had before him the beginning of the second Feeding in Mt. (xv. 29), "and he went up into the mountain and sat there." He tells us almost word for word: "And Jesus went up into the mountain, and there he sat with his disciples." At the second place, however, when he was about to pass from the Feeding to Jesus' walking on the sea (vi. 15) he remembered that Mk. and Mt., in their first story of the Feeding, said that between the two acts Jesus ascended the mountain (his language agrees very closely with Mt. xiv. 23), and so he added this and overlooked the fact that he had said nothing about Jesus coming down. For another example see xx. 2 (chap. iii., 26). In i. 15, in the words, "This was he of whom I said, He that cometh after me is become before me,'" the Baptist actually recalls something he has said about Jesus at an earlier date, but which is not found in the Fourth Gospel but only in the Synoptics Mt. iii. 11), though there the language and meaning are different.

4. Is JN.'S PURPOSE SIMPLY TO SUPPLEMENT AND CORRECT?

But why does Jn. differ so often from the Synoptics, if he was acquainted with their books? The most important attempt to explain this consists in saying that his purpose throughout his book is to supplement the story of his predecessors and, where in small matters this was inexact, to correct it. This theory therefore presupposes further that he was himself present at the events described, and was entitled to think that wherever he made additions and corrections he was justified in doing so. Whether this is confirmed is a question we shall soon have to investigate more closely. We leave it for the present and simply ask, Can this double purpose, which is ascribed to him, be discovered at all in his book? As regards this intention to make corrections, it is certainly not easy to recognise it, for the author nowhere says: the matter was not thus, but thus. If then he made corrections, he must have made them quite quietly out of respect for his predecessors.

We prefer, therefore, in the first instance, to consider the question: Does he wish merely to give facts which are supplementary? In the case of the narratives which are peculiar to him, this would be conceivable, as well as in the case of the expulsion of the dealers from the fore-court of the Temple, if such an event really took place at the beginning of Jesus' ministry. But in Jn. we find again a number of stories given by the Synoptics, in which the idea cannot possibly be that the events happened a second time, and not merely on one occasion as the Synoptics state. We need only mention the Feeding of the Five Thousand, the walking on the sea and the entrance into Jerusalem (vi. 1-15, 16-21; xii. 12-16). It might really be thought in the case of the second of these stories that the idea of correcting was the ruling purpose; Jn., in opposition to the story of the Synoptics which says that Jesus was taken into the boat in the middle of the sea, wishes, as an eye witness, to insist that this was not so, since Jesus crossed the lake from one shore to the other. But it is really hard to discover what correction he means to make in his description of the entry into Jerusalem, or, in particular, in that of the Feeding of the Five Thousand; and this is sufficient to show that the whole idea that Jn.'s purpose is always either to supplement or correct is untenable. If, on the other hand, certain concessions are made, and it is claimed that he only meant to do this now arid then, the whole explanation of the passages in which he differs from the Synoptics would have no value; for in the case of a considerable number of sections in his book the question why he introduced them would still be left unexplained.

5. JN.'S PURPOSE NOT MERELY TO SUPPLEMENT AND CORRECT.

But let us see rather more exactly how in detail people think of the author as carrying out his purpose of supplementing and correcting the Synoptics. Here special importance may be attached to his statement that some time after Jesus' public appearance John the Baptist was still baptizing and that Jesus was doing so too, and to the addition, "for John was not yet imprisoned" (iii. 22-24). In the Synoptics (Mk. i. 14), Jesus does not come forward publicly until after the imprisonment of the Baptist. Consequently the remark in Jn. which contradicts this might easily be due in this instance to his purpose of making a correction. If this were so, Jn. is aware, as the Synoptics are not, that Jesus started a public mission while the Baptist was still at work. And here we should have the explanation of the fact that he adds so much which these omit: all this really happened before the arrest of the Baptist, with which in the Synoptics the story of Jesus work begins.

All? Strictly speaking, as a matter of fact, everything that Jn. reports; for he never mentions a point at which the Baptist was imprisoned. But this view of the matter would be quite impossible; for in the expression "not yet taken" Jn. betrays the fact that he knew very well of the arrest of the Baptist, and thinks of it as happening during the public ministry of Jesus. But when? Before v. 35 ("he was the lamp") and certainly before the Feeding of the Five Thousand and Jesus' walking on the sea (Jn. vi. 1-21), of which the Synoptics do not speak until long after the imprisonment of the Baptist--unless we were to adopt the quite untenable assumption (see p. 48) that Jn. in these two stories is thinking of two events quite different from those the Synoptics have in mind. But we find afterwards in Jn. (chap. vii.-xi.) Jesus appearing in Jerusalem at the Feast of Tabernacles, the cure of the man born blind, Jesus appearing at the Feast of the Dedication of the Temple, and the raising of Lazarus--all things about which the Synoptics say nothing, and which, nevertheless, are so extremely important, that their silence about them is quite inexplicable. In all these cases it does not help us at all to be told that Jn. merely wished to supply facts as to what happened before the imprisonment of the Baptist.

At the best, therefore, the assumption could be used for the events which Jn. narrates in chapters ii.-v. But before we adopt it, we shall do well once more to examine closely the passage on which it is based. "Jesus baptized," we are told in Jn. iii. 22 (26; iv. 1). And in iv. 2 we read "and yet Jesus himself baptized not, but his disciples." What would a writer, who was anxious to report nothing false, have done when he noticed afterwards that this had happened? We may be sure that he would afterwards have deleted the error in the earlier passage, instead of allowing it to stand and appending the confession that he had made a mistake. Here we can see the peculiar character of the Fourth Evangelist. He is not an author who is anxious to report nothing false; where it suits his purpose, he reports it.

And here in fact it suits his purpose very well. It is only the statement, that Jesus baptized, and did so while John was still at work, that enables him to represent the interesting situation in which the number of the followers of the Baptist is becoming smaller and smaller, and that of the followers of Jesus growing larger and larger. And this is one of Jn.'s chief aims. "He must increase, but I must decrease" (iii. 30): with these words the Baptist himself is made to write the legend to this little picture, which is really sketched very gracefully. In order to do so, the author adds a touch which, in reality, as he himself knows, does not at all harmonise with the truth.

Only one? Of course the picture includes that other feature we have mentioned; John the Baptist is still at large. Must we see in this a correct addition, a correction made by an eye-witness when the same "eye-witness" in another verse not far off has told us with equal precision something which on his own admission is not true? Must we base upon this our idea of the purpose of correction which he followed throughout his book? A different idea of his purpose has resulted, with an incomparably greater amount of probability, from this very example; he wishes to be not a reporter who is to be taken at his word, but a painter; a painter of vivid scenes designed to make clear and impressive a higher truth--in the present instance the truth that John was only the forerunner of Jesus, and had to take an entirely subordinate place, in fact does so of his own free will. And if we now ask again, how long the Evangelist imagines the Baptist to be still at large while Jesus is at work, the only answer can be: merely for this particular scene, and not for those that follow. Once his retirement before Jesus has been described, the Baptist is so unimportant to Jn. that he does not think his arrest worth reporting. Indeed, even in the case of preceding events (the marriage at Cana, the expulsion of the dealers from the fore-court of the Temple, the conversation with Nicodemus), he seems to have hardly thought that they occurred while the Baptist was still at large.

But the theory that Jn. wishes to supplement the Synoptics by giving the earliest events in the public life of Jesus is overthrown by what we are told as regards the discourses of Jesus, when it is presupposed that these also served the purpose of supplementing the Synoptics. If Jesus be supposed to have spoken in both ways--as he is represented as doing in the Synoptics and as Jn. makes him do--it cannot be imagined that the style met with in Jn. was the earlier. We are told on the contrary that Jn. preserves the manner of speech in which Jesus addressed his disciples in his last days, after he had finished his ministry amongst the people, which latter is reflected in his discourses in the Synoptics. This statement might seem worth considering if the discourses of Jesus preserved to us in Jn. were solely farewell ad dresses to his disciples during his last days, like those in chapters xiii.-xvii. But, as a matter of fact, Jn. represents Jesus as speaking from the very beginning in the same style as in these farewell discourses. To sum up, in the events which he describes, Jn. is supposed to take us back to the earliest days, and in the discourses which Jesus delivered at these, the earliest events in his public career, this same author Jn. is supposed to preserve the tone in which Jesus spoke during the last weeks of his life. Both assumptions are necessary if we are to insist that Jn. wishes to supplement and correct the Synoptics. And yet one of the two assumptions annuls the other.

6. ARE SEVERAL JOURNEYS OF JESUS TO JERUSALEM PRESUPPOSED IN MT. xxiii. 37?

But an attempt is made in another way to show that Jn. could not really be in conflict with his predecessors. Those who make it find in the Synoptics themselves passages here and there which confirm, as they think, the story of Jn. In particular, several journeys of Jesus to Jerusalem, connected with a public appearance there, are, they say, presupposed when Jesus says in Mt. (xxiii. 37): "Jerusalem, Jerusalem, that killest the prophets, and stonest them that are sent unto thee, how often would I have gathered thy children together, even as a hen gathereth her chickens under her wings, and ye would not." The inference really appears to be unavoidable. The only remarkable thing is that the Synoptists themselves have not drawn it. If they themselves really suggest that Jesus came forward so often in Jerusalem, why do they not only tell us nothing about this, but represent things as if when he made this utterance he had come to Jerusalem for the first time to counsel and admonish. Thus those who refer to this utterance as a corroboration of the story of Jn. are producing a greater puzzle as regards the Synoptists, who likewise claim that their story has a right to be regarded as correct. So that before we attach such great importance to the utterance in question, we prefer to examine it again more closely.

When we do this, it is clear in the very first instance that it does not read as people think it does, and in the way in which we have rendered it above, intentionally following the general practice, in order to show what mistakes one is liable to make when one follows a popular custom. In reality--and in Lk. (xiii. 34) exactly as in Mt.--it reads: "Jerusalem, Jerusalem, that kills the prophets and stones them that are sent unto her, how often would I have gathered thy children," &c. Jerusalem is therefore apostrophised only in the second half of the sentence; in the first something is said about the city without the city itself being addressed. No one who has a thought clearly in his mind, and intends to write it down in an equally simple sentence, would express himself in this way.

On the other hand, the remarkable form of the sentence would be quite intelligible if our Evangelists, Mt. and Lk., or rather the earlier writer from whom they both draw, [3] used a book in which the sentence about Jerusalem appeared without any apostrophe; and if they or he proceeded to introduce the apostrophe without noticing that, having made this alteration, the sentence should have been made to read differently at the beginning. And this is not a mere conjecture; we have, in addition, a clue which indicates the kind of book it may have been. In Mt., that is to say, the utterance immediately follows another (xxiii. 34-36) to this effect: "Therefore, behold, I send unto you prophets, and wise men, and scribes; some of them shall ye kill and crucify, and some of them shall ye scourge in your synagogues, and persecute from city to city," &c. Lk. gives this utterance in xi. 49-51, keeping the continuation about Jerusalem--quoted above--for chap. xiii. of his book. But this earlier utterance in Lk. not only dispenses with the apostrophe, as the beginning of the continuation about Jerusalem does--"I will send unto them prophets and apostles, and some of them they shall kill and persecute," &c.--but--and this is the chief point it is preceded by the introductory words: u There fore also said the wisdom of God."

The Wisdom of God is represented in several books of the Old Testament as a person who takes up the word (Prov. viii. f., Ecclus. xxiv.), or is found as the title of a book (Wisdom of Solomon; Wisdom of Jesus, son of Sirach). The saying under consideration is not found in any of these books. But it is clear that it cannot have been framed for the first time by Jesus. In what precedes Jesus is addressing the Pharisees. He could not, therefore, as he does in Lk., suddenly continue, "therefore also said the wisdom of God," unless what now follows is a saying which was already well known. But this is clear from the version in Mt. as well, though here the introductory formula is wanting. Jesus cannot have said of himself, as Mt. makes him say, "I send to you prophets and wise men and Scribes," for he never did this, and at least would never have sent Scribes, whose attitude towards him was so unfriendly. Lk. knew very well what he was doing, when he substituted "Prophets and Apostles"; for Jesus could really send Apostles and (New Testament) Prophets. In this description of the persons sent, Mt. therefore has, we may be sure, preserved the more original version, but in the introductory formula it is Lk. who has done so. In Mt. the only remaining clue to the fact that his predecessor had before him a book in which this introductory formula stood is the word "therefore."

But what kind of book was it? If the Scribes were mentioned amongst those men who were sent by God to the people, it was the work of a pious Jew who reproached his people for being stiff-necked, and was anxious to induce them to repent. Whether it had the title "Wisdom"--perhaps with some addition-- or whether Wisdom was simply represented as speaking in it, we do not know. From this book, according to the story of the predecessor of our Mt. and Lk., Jesus quoted a passage in support of his own words in which he warned the Pharisees that they would be punished. In this way it is still used in Lk. Mt., on the other hand, has wrongly understood it and introduced it in such a way that Jesus uses the words as his own, and Lk. also, as regards the utterance about Jerusalem, shares the misunderstanding. Thus it was the Wisdom of God which said that it had often wished to gather together Jerusalem's children, as a hen gathers her chickens. This it had actually done by sending prophets and wise men and Scribes. It is not Jesus who says he has done this. Thus the whole confirmation of Jn.'s story of many visits of Jesus to Jerusalem rests solely on the fact that an utterance put into the mouth of the Wisdom of God by a Jewish author has been wrongly regarded as a saying of Jesus. And now we understand also why the Synoptics, in spite of this "saying of Jesus" in which he says how often he has concerned himself about Jerusalem, had no information about these labours.

7. IS JESUS' RELATIONSHIP TO GOD IN MT. xi. 27 THE SAME AS IN JN.?

It would be still more important if we could find a second passage in the Synoptics fitted to confirm the story of Jn. We mean such confirmation as would relate not merely to one particular point, such as the journeys of Jesus to Jerusalem, but to the whole character of Jesus' discourses. We have in mind Mt. xi. 27: "All things have been delivered unto me of my Father, and no one knoweth the Son, save the Father; neither (doth any know) the Father, save the Son, and he to whomsoever the Son willeth to reveal him." These words seem certainly to be spoken quite in the spirit of the Fourth Gospel, which in x. 14 f., for instance, says ("I am the good shepherd; and I know mine own, and mine own know me), even as the Father knoweth me, and I know the Father." In Jn. this mutual knowledge must be understood in the sense that Jesus had from eternity existed with God in heaven before he came down to earth.

Now it is certainly remarkable that in the Synoptics only this one saying can be found which gives expression to this thought, and might be compared to the discourses of Jesus in Jn. If, as is claimed, it really implies confirmation of these, again all that we get is a new puzzle as regards the Synoptics: why in these does Jesus not speak in this way more often, instead of talking everywhere else in such an entirely different way? This consideration obliges us to re-examine the utterance more closely.

This also originally read quite differently. All ecclesiastical and heretical writers of the second century, who give us any information about this passage, entirely or in part support the following version: "All things have been delivered unto me of my Father, and no one hath known the Father, save the Son, neither the Son save the Father, and he to whomsoever the Son willeth to reveal him."

Even the Church Father, Irenaeus, about A.D. 185, who warmly upbraids a Christian sect for making use of this version, follows it several times in his writings; it must therefore have really been found in his own Bible. As compared with it, the version which we now have in the Bible cannot under any circumstances claim the preference. It is true that our oldest copies of the Bible contain it, but they are about two centuries later than the authorities we have mentioned. And no plausible reason can be given why the version current in the second century should be due to a deliberate change on the part of a Christian sect; on the other hand, since the one form must have arisen through an alteration of the other, it is very conceivable that it is the text in our present Bible which has resulted from a change, because, we may suppose, the writer was anxious to make the language resemble more closely Jesus style of preaching in Jn.

Is the difference so great then? At first sight it might seem slight. But that is a very wrong impression. While we read, "No one knoweth the Son . . . the Father," a mutual knowledge from eternity may be meant, and, as we said just now, this is one of the ideas of the Fourth Gospel. When, however, we read, "no one hath known," a definite point of time is fixed at which the knowledge first began; and when Jesus goes on to say of himself, "no one has known the Father but the Son," it is clear that the knowledge of the Father cannot have commenced before some definite date in his earthly life, since the Synoptics are not aware that Jesus existed in heaven before he lived on earth. Nevertheless, if the words in the first place were, "no one hath known the Son save the Father," it would still be possible that at any rate the knowledge on the part of God was present from eternity, and this would be in agreement with the style of thought in the Fourth Gospel. But a second important peculiarity in the oldest version is found in this very fact that the first place is assigned to the clause, "No one hath known the Father save the Son," and that the other clause follows, "No one hath known the Son, save the Father." And since the knowledge spoken of first was not gained earlier than during the earthly life of Jesus, we cannot suppose that the knowledge referred to in the second clause belongs to an earlier date.

The meaning is really quite simple: Jesus alone has acquired the knowledge that God is not a Lord who is jealous for his own honour, and cannot be approached by men, but is a loving Father. This of itself means that he can feel himself to be a son of God. It is a feeling of his own, however, which no one so far has realised--none of his hearers, but God alone. This second part of the thought is very well expressed in Lk. (x. 22) by the clause: "no one knows (more correctly, has known) who the son is," that is to say, that I am he. Finally, with this agrees very well the conclusion in Mt. and Lk., "and to whom the son will reveal it." In the usual version of the saying, the immediately preceding words are: "no one knows the Father, but the son." What the latter will reveal is thus the deeper nature of God, and, understood in the spirit of the Fourth Gospel, the meaning might be that Jesus acquired the knowledge during his pre-existence in heaven. But, according to the correct version, the immediately preceding words are, "no one has known the son, but the Father," and here the following words mean, "and he to whom I myself am willing to reveal that I am that son; you have all failed as yet to recognise this, I myself must tell you of it."

Strictly speaking, when the knowledge that God is the Father dawns upon any man, he can feel that he himself is His son; this knowledge Jesus wished to bring to all, and said, "blessed are the peacemakers, for they shall be called the sons of God," "love your enemies, and pray for them that persecute you, that ye may be sons of your Father which is in heaven" (Mt. v. 9, 44 f.). He used the expression "sons of God," and so the same expression as he applied to himself. Instead of this, Jn. continually uses of men--and he is the first to do so--the phrase "children of God," reserving the expression "Son of God" for Jesus alone, and Luther, without any justification, has used it also in Mt. and in other places where the original has "sons." [4] It is quite clear that, in view of what we have said, Jesus cannot have called himself Son of God in a sense that only applies to himself, on the ground, for instance, that he proceeded from God in a manner different from that in which human beings come into existence at their birth; he can only have done so in a sense in which all men can become what he was, that is to say, sons of God who are equally ready to obey absolutely the Father in heaven, but at the same time rely upon His love, just as a human son relies upon the love of his human father. If we of to-day wish to express the sense in which Jesus called himself Son of God in a way that cannot be misunderstood, we must do the reverse of what Jn. has done--use the other expression and say that Jesus felt himself to be a child of God.

Turning again to Mt. xi. 27, we must remember that at this time Jesus alone possessed the knowledge that God is a loving Father. This made him singular and raised him above other men. Thus the thought of being God's son made him feel in addition that he was sent by God to reveal this knowledge to his brethren. This is the meaning of the initial words of the saying: "all things have been delivered to me of my Father." It does not imply any super human power, as in the saying (which, it is almost generally agreed, was not spoken by Jesus), "all power is given to me in heaven and upon earth" (Mt. xxviii. 18). Here the word "power" does occur in the passage, but not in the text under consideration. What is delivered to Jesus, in our passage, we must gather simply from the context; on the evidence of the saying itself, it is the knowledge that we can regard God as our Father. In agreement with this is the fact that according to xi. 25 it must be something which was hidden from the wise and revealed to the simple, and according to xi. 28-30 something which was quite different from the yoke of the Jewish Law under which the weary and heavy-laden groaned, while Jesus yoke was easy and his burden light, and was able to refresh the soul because it consisted simply in doing the will of God gladly and in relying upon His love.

Are all these thoughts similar to those found in the Fourth Gospel? Far from it. On the contrary, no utterance harmonises with the spirit of Jesus' discourses in the Synoptics so well as the one we have been considering if we hold fast to its original language. In fact, it is precisely this that enables us for the first time to under stand fully how Jesus came to be what he was according to the Synoptics; at first he was quite simply a man who in the course of his mental development realised that he had a Father in heaven; next he became one who felt himself called by this Father of his to be a leader, sent to the people, because he found that he stood quite alone in having this knowledge, and yet could not be silent about it; and from this it was easy to take a further step and to feel obliged to regard himself as that highest messenger sent by God, whom his people and his age thought of as the one who had been long promised, as the Messiah.

8. INACCURATE RECOLLECTION ON THE PART OF THE APOSTLE JOHN?

What remains, if we still wish to maintain that the Fourth Gospel is in agreement with the first three? If we disregard various other expedients, which are far less likely to be satisfactory than those we have already discussed, there is only one left. We are told by the Church Fathers that at the end of the first century the Apostle John was still living. This being so, it is eagerly assumed that he did not write his gospel until shortly before his death. And whereas his great age obscured his recollection of many matters in the life of Jesus, he remembered other things quite correctly. This explains, it is said, how it is that his book, apart from much that is incorrect, contains much that serves to correct the story of the Synoptics.

In itself this assumption has nothing impossible about it; if indeed it could be accepted that the Gospel was composed by the apostle and in his old age, this theory might be deemed fairly probable. Since, however, we must first examine the two presuppositions on which it is based, let us at the outset put the simple question, What would the result be? At least not this--that Jn., as compared with the Synoptics, must always be regarded as everywhere right. This particular idea therefore is abandoned as being untenable. To what extent is he right then? To suit the real desire of those who put forward this theory, he is right on as many points as possible. For the main purpose of these people is to support the idea that we have in Jn. the work of an eye-witness of the life of Jesus. But when we examine the matter more closely, his trustworthiness is abandoned on one point after another, because, however much we may wish to believe in it, it cannot be maintained.

In particular, as regards the discourses of Jesus, it is more and more generally conceded that it was the aged John who first conceived them in the style in which they appear in the Fourth Gospel. His conception of Jesus changed in the course of his long life, and as these new ideas took shape his recollection of the discourses of Jesus altered as well. If this were assumed to a moderate extent, it might seem conceivable; but people would never have jumped at so doubtful an expedient, unless the difference between Jn.'s style of discourse and the other style, which may really be accepted as original, were very marked indeed.

Thus the result of emphasising the great age of John is really the opposite of what was intended. The desire was simply to defend the trustworthiness of the Fourth Gospel as against the Synoptics, and yet the would-be defenders are obliged in a clear, if rather veiled, manner to admit that on most points he is untrustworthy.

We have now come to the end of the attempts to reconcile the accounts of the life of Jesus in the Synoptics and in Jn. In conclusion, we can only say that we sincerely pity any one who engages in this labour. If on many particular points his efforts seem to be really satisfactory to him, he can never rejoice at his success; for he has no sooner shown that it is not absolutely impossible to reconcile some new little circumstance in Jn. with the Synoptics than a whole series of others come to light which defy every attempt at reconciliation.

Footnotes:

3. The truth of the theory that they had the work of an earlier writer before them has been fully demonstrated. Cp. Wernle, Die Quellen des Lelens Jesu, pp. 70-7-4 (in the Religionsgeschichtlichen Volksbücher; Engl. trans, pp. 131-139).

4. Paul interchanges "sons" and "children" without any distinction. Luther renders only the Singular by "son" (Heb. xii. 5-7; Rev. xxi. 7), the Plural by "sons" only in the phrase "sons and daughters" (2 Cor. vi. 18). In Gal. iv. 7 he arbitrarily changes the Singular into the Plural in order to be able to use the term "children." The Authorised English Version has, like Luther, son for the Singular, but also in Gal. iv. 7. For the Plural it has in half the cases sons (Rom. viii. 14, 19; Gal. iv. 6; Heb. ii. 10, xii. 7 f.; besides 2 Cor. vi. 18), but in the other half, like Luther, children (Mt. v. 9, 45; Lk. vi. 35, xx. 36; Rom. ix. 26; Gal. iii. 26; Heb. xii. 5). The Revised Version everywhere translates correctly son or sons.

CHAPTER III - DECISION AS TO WHICH IS THE MORE TRUST WORTHY: THE STORY OF THE FIRST THREE GOSPELS OR OF THE FOURTH?

WE have then to make a choice. And from what has already been said we are not as yet precluded from giving decided preference to Jn.

1. REASONS FOR FAVOURING JN.

Beyond question there are people who think such a picture of Jesus as the Fourth Gospel gives not merely beautiful in the sense in which even a fairy-tale may be felt to be beautiful, but also more trustworthy than that of the Synoptics. They are not concerned to find Jesus humanly intelligible in his whole character; on the contrary, the less human it is, the truer does it seem to them to be. It is not merely that they want one who can do the greatest miracles, but they really think it a most likely thing that, when the time was fulfilled, God would have caused exactly such a Saviour to appear. They are not disturbed when they find that Jesus' enemies, in spite of all their efforts, never succeeded in overpowering him, and think it quite natural that the attempts did not succeed because God tied their hands. It does not surprise them that Jesus spoke to the people about his coming from heaven in a way that they could not under stand at all; were his teaching intelligible, it seems to them it would not have been so sublime as it must certainly have been. Taking examples from history, we will only add that Clement of Alexandria as early as about A.D. 200 called the Gospel of John the pneumatic Gospel, that Luther called it the true, unique, tender Gospel of Gospels, and that Schleiermacher (ob. 1834) ranked it high above the Synoptics.

We have no idea of arguing with people who feel in this way. We do not wish to destroy their idea; we respect it. One thing, however, they cannot expect us to attribute to them--we mean, the historical sense. Every one who has had much to do with history knows that, to understand events and characters, it is of the first importance to look for such explanations as suggest themselves to us from experience of other human happenings. There will always be points which we cannot clear up in this way. But every student of history knows that he would be defeating his own purpose if he were to set aside those obvious explanations which hold good again and again in all human experience and were to try to put in place of them indefinite and unusual explanations, such as a miracle, a direct intervention on the part of God. In other branches of history, even those people whom we have described above carefully avoid this; it is only in the field of "sacred" history that they prefer the dark to the clear, the inconceivable to the conceivable, the miraculous to the natural.

2. PREFERENCE FOR THE SYNOPTICS ON THE WHOLE.

When we address our question, Do the Synoptics or Jn. deserve the preference? to those who do not care to make such a distinction between "sacred" and ordinary human history, who, though they are quite prepared to find in the history of Jesus and especially in his inmost character much that is unfathomable, would like even here to see as much that is clear and humanly intelligible as it is possible to see, we are almost inclined to conjecture that the decision has already been made. Much as we have tried, in enumerating the distinctions between the two stories of the life of Jesus, to make the facts alone speak, we could not help it if these made the scale turn in favour of the Synoptics: and the review of the attempts which have been made to reconcile the two accounts could hardly fail to strengthen this impression.

Our task is now therefore merely to sum up the matter as briefly as possible, and then to give a rather more detailed treatment of some further points in which the trustworthiness of Jn. really needs to be more thoroughly investigated or in which it is still necessary to explain how it is that Jn. has come to make statements differing so widely from the truth. When we do this it will be time to say plainly what we think of these statements, whereas so far we have refrained from doing so, and have faithfully followed our purpose of giving in the first instance only the facts (p. 4).

3. INFLUENCE OF JESUS WITH HIS HEARERS.

Which is more likely--that Jesus came into contact with all sorts and conditions of men amongst his people and achieved successes of every kind, or that he had to deal almost entirely and without distinction with the "Jews" in a body? Which is more likely that he often had an enthusiastic reception, or that the Jews, in a compact body, refused to believe in him? It is said in Jn. often enough that "many" believed in him on this or that occasion (ii. 23; vii. 31; viii. 30; x. 42, &c.). This, however, should not deceive us as to the fact, that as a general result the Jews do not believe. When a certain number believe, this always (apart from x. 42) gives rise to a division among Jesus' hearers, and if that had not happened, Jesus would never have been led to speak such words as "if a man keep my word, he shall never see death" (viii. 51) and the like, which Jn. is determined to record. But the belief has no permanent result, for when Jesus delivers his farewell discourses (chaps. xiii.-xvii.), only the little band of his intimate disciples is represented as being still true to him; all those who have believed only for a time are referred to in the saying: "But Jesus did not trust himself unto them, for that he knew all men" (ii. 24); in other words, he knew that in the end these--all of them--would join in the cry, "Crucify him, crucify him" (xix. 6, 15).

4. COURSE OF JESUS' PUBLIC WORK.

But if from the first Jesus really met with so much hostility, how are we to understand why he was so long allowed such freedom? Is it conceivable that, after driving the dealers from the fore-court of the Temple, and supposing that it took place at the beginning of his visits to Jerusalem, he could have continued to work for two years unmolested? In Galilee, it would be easier to think this; it is not so easy to imagine that he could have done so under the eyes of the Jewish authorities in Jerusalem, where, according to Jn., he stayed with few exceptions. The excuse that "his hour was not yet come" (vii. 30; viii. 20), is one which, having regard to all we know from the rest of human history, should be characterised as quite unsatisfactory.

5. JESUS' STYLE OF SPEAKING.

But if Jesus really met with a friendly reception and had a following, especially amongst the humble and oppressed members of his race--and no one would like to give up the idea that he had-- which is the more likely, that this success was due to the style of addresses the Synoptics describe him as giving to the people or to that which Jn. describes? In the Synoptics he really lifts from the people the heavy yoke of the Old Testament law with its thousand impossible precepts, and substitutes the light yoke of a free, childlike obedience to the simple command to love God and one's neighbour; in Jn., instead of this, we find nothing but an incessant command, supported by bare assurances and awe-inspiring miracles, to believe in him and his coming from heaven. It was really difficult for a soul in anguish to derive any comfort from it. There is certainly nothing more touching to such a soul known to any one--not even to the worshippers of the Jesus of the Fourth Gospel--than the parable of the Prodigal Son (Lk. xv. 11-32), whom the father, in spite of his great fault, goes forth to meet and embrace when he comes back penitent to his old home. This parable, with those of the Good Samaritan (Lk. x. 25-37), of the cruel and wicked servant (Mt. xviii. 23-35), of the Pharisee and the Publican (Lk. xviii. 9-14), and all the others, so helpful and dear to us as precious and living examples of a simple piety which at once touches the heart, we seek for in vain in the "true, unique, tender Gospel of Gospels"--and not because they are already found in the Synoptics and must not be repeated, but because they do not illustrate the only matter about which the Jesus of Jn. is permitted to speak, his divine majesty.

6. MISUNDERSTANDINGS AS REGARDS JESUS' DISCOURSES.

We have reached a point at which we may also say that it is not the hearers of Jesus who are to be accused of having seriously misunderstood his discourses, and that it was not Jesus who intentionally provoked the misunderstandings. The author himself inserts in Jesus' discourses, when they have, as a matter of fact, already reached their end, some expression having more meanings than one, in order that he may proceed to tell us how, when the hearers of Jesus understood him in an external, material sense, he explained his deeper, spiritual meaning, and in so doing brought to light on the one hand a want of intelligence on the part of the people, and even of the disciples, and on the other the unsuspected profundity of his own disclosures. These misunderstandings are not therefore the reminiscences of an eye-witness, but a device employed by the author.

7. REPETITIONS IN JESUS' DISCOURSES.

When we consider further how limited a number of ideas are continually repeated in these discourses in a way which is felt to be quite monotonous and tedious even by very many of those who regard the Fourth Gospel with a kind of awe, we wonder the more how Jesus could have gone on talking in this way for two years without being left with no one at all to listen to him.

But we have still to add something which has not so far been mentioned: in Jn. Jesus continues a discourse even when in the meantime a series of events have happened, and when of course the audience has changed. He says, for example, at the Feast of the Dedication of the Temple (x. 26; cp. 22), "But ye believe not, because ye are not of my sheep," and then proceeds to enlarge upon the idea of the sheep, just as he has done on an earlier and quite different occasion (x. 3, 10 f., 14). On another occasion, at the Feast of Tabernacles (vii. 23; cp. 2) he says, "are ye wroth with me, because I made a man every whit whole on the Sabbath? "Now the only act of the kind which has been mentioned so far is the healing of the sick man at Bethesda (v. 1-16) which took place at an earlier, but not definitely distinguished, "feast of the Jews." Since this, according to Jn., Jesus fed the Five Thousand at the Passover Feast in Galilee (vi. 4), and the interval between this and the Feast of Tabernacles would amount to another six months.

8. LEAVES IN JN. WRONGLY ARRANGED

That, in spite of this, he should speak as if the healing at Bethesda had only just happened is so striking as to have given rise to the theory that the page which contained this continuation of the discourse got shifted in Jn.'s manuscript or in one of the oldest copies of it, from its proper place in the book, and was reinserted in a wrong place farther back. This is not in itself impossible; indeed, the existence of this kind of mistake in several ancient books has been made so probable that there can no longer be any question about it. Of course, if it occurred here, both the first words and the last in the wrongly inserted leaf must have caused some disturbance in the context of the book, and in the place where the leaf originally stood a lacuna in the narrative, as we have it, would be noticeable. But there is nothing of this in the passage under consideration; and, apart from this, there are very many other passages, in which, because the order of events is unlikely, or because the order in the Gospel of Jn. does not agree with that of the Synoptics, one would like to suppose that a leaf has been misplaced in some such manner. We wish any one who proposes by such expedients to bring the Fourth Gospel into good order and into agreement with the Synoptics a long life, but his labour is one which will never suffice for his task.

9. CARELESS DESCRIPTION IN JN.

The matter is much simpler. As we found in the case of the misunderstandings, it is not Jesus but the Evangelist who enlarges upon the ideas and spins out the discourses. He imagines Jesus as having always the same hearers, because he has no real recollection of actual cases in which Jesus confronted the people. It is his fault, and not the fault of Jesus, that no account is taken of the intervals which must have elapsed between two of Jesus utterances which could not have been so close together in actual life as they are on paper.

This explains further how it is that the discourses of Jesus and the remarks of the Evangelist himself are often so much alike that the one might be taken for the other--they are even amalgamated with the discourses of the Baptist. In the midst of one of these a number of utterances begins in iii. 31, of a kind that only Jesus himself makes elsewhere in the Fourth Gospel, and yet it is not said that Jesus is the speaker. The expositors are therefore quite at a loss to know whether to ascribe them to the Baptist or to regard them as remarks of the Evangelist himself. Even the well-known saying, "And this is life eternal, that they should know thee the only true God, and him whom thou didst send, even Jesus Christ," is in Jn. (xvii. 3) an utterance made by Jesus himself, though, were it his, he would surely have said, "and know me whom thou hast sent," especially as he is using the words in a prayer addressed to God.

In these cases there is certainly a considerable amount of carelessness on the part of the Evangelist. But the most friendly critic cannot deny that there is evidence of it in other places as well. At the beginning of the story of the raising of Lazarus, Jn. mentions (xi. 1 f.) Lazarus sisters Martha and Mary, and adds: "And it was that Mary which anointed the Lord with ointment, and wiped his feet with her hair." We ask in vain where Jn. has already narrated this. There would perhaps be some excuse--though it would still be strange--if he thought he might refer to Mary in this way because the description of the anointing was known to his readers from the older Gospels (cp. i. 15, p. 52). In that case his purpose would be to add, as a new point, that the woman who is mentioned in the Synoptics but is not named was no other than this same Mary. But we do not find in any of the Synoptics what seems to be recalled here. According to Mk. (xiv. 3) and Mt. (xxvi. 7), a woman in Bethany, near Jerusalem, pours the contents of a flask of precious nard, having according to Mk. broken it for the purpose, on Jesus head. According to Lk. (vii. 37 f.), when Jesus was invited in Galilee to sup at the house of a Pharisee, a sinful woman of the town moistened his feet with her tears, dried them with her hair, kissed them, and anointed them with ointment. Which of these accounts does Jn. wish to recall to us? Neither meets the case. On the other hand, the puzzle is solved at once when we reach the 12th chapter of his own Gospel. Here in v. 3 we are told for the first time something which is already referred to in chap. xi. as a past event (see further, below pp. 81-83). Here Jn. tells us distinctly that what is narrated in the 12th chapter happened later than what he has reported in the 11th chapter. If a modern writer were to tell us something like this, we should think ourselves badly treated, and would not easily forgive him.

10. COLOURLESS DESCRIPTIONS IN JN.

Further, in how colourless a way many of the scenes in Jn. are sketched! Certain Greeks come (xii. 20) to Jerusalem for the Passover Feast and wish to see Jesus. They apply to Philip; he tells Andrew, and both inform Jesus. Up to this point every word suggests that we are dealing with an eye-witness, so precise is every statement. And then? "But Jesus answered them" (i.e. the two disciples), "the hour is come that the Son of Man should be glorified," &c. He makes a reference to his impending death, to which he cheerfully reconciles himself. Whether the Greeks were admitted to see him, what they said, what Jesus said to them--about all this we hear nothing. Similarly, the conversation with Nicodemus, to take another example (iii. 1-21), has no conclusion. It is again clear that the author is not concerned about the persons who come into touch with Jesus, but entirely about Jesus himself.

11. THE PICTURE OF JOHN THE BAPTIST.

Even John the Baptist has suffered the same fate. In the Synoptics he conies before us a character which of itself would have a claim to interest us greatly, even if it had never been brought into close touch with Jesus. The purpose of his baptism and preaching of repentance, and their benefit to the people, would have been achieved in any case. It is not merely his pathetic death (Mk. vi. 17-29) that makes him sure of winning the sympathy of readers of the Synoptics, but also his uncertainty as to whether he is to regard Jesus as the Messiah (Mt. xi. 2 f.). It shows how truly Jesus speaks when he says that he is greater than any Old Testament figure, and yet least amongst the New Testament believers (Mt. xi. 11). He could call men to repentance, but he had not himself been commissioned to preach the glad tidings. We are told only in Mt. (iii. 14 f.) that he refused to baptize Jesus, and this is clearly a later touch, for according to the most original account which we can still gather easily from Mk., he did not learn Jesus higher nature even at the baptism itself. Jesus alone in Mk. (i. 10) sees the heavens open and the Holy Spirit coming down upon him like a dove. And this is undoubtedly the correct version, since no one would have invented it, if as Lk. reports (iii. 21 f.), and as regards the heavens Mt. also (iii. 16), the opening of the heavens and the coming down of the spirit were visible to every one. It is true that Mk. also (like Mt. and Lk.), as regards the voice from heaven, only says that it sounded, which seems to imply that it could be heard by every one. But only Mt. says "this is my beloved son, in whom I am well pleased;" Mk. (and Lk.), on the contrary, "thou art," &c.; and from this we may certainly assume that according to the older account which was used by Mk., the voice could be heard by Jesus alone, just as he alone saw the heavens open.

In the Fourth Gospel, however, the Baptist knows from the beginning not only of Jesus higher nature, as in Mt., and that he was destined to be the Redeemer of the whole world (i. 27, 29), but also that he pre-existed with God in heaven (i. 15, 30). But for this very reason the work of the Baptist is strictly limited: he bears witness to Jesus (i. 6-8, 15, 23). His baptism is never of any importance to those who receive it. John uses it only as a means of testifying to Jesus (i. 26, 31). His preaching of repentance is not even mentioned. It would thus be quite impossible for him to ask later whether Jesus is the Messiah, as in Mt. xi. 2 f., unless we were to explain such a question by ascribing to him doubts-- which would be quite sinful--of all that had been revealed to him at an earlier date by God Himself, According to the original account of the Synoptics, on the other hand, he had as yet no actual knowledge which would enable him to answer the question. In short, in place of a character which was full of power, if limited in its spiritual outlook, and of a person whose tragic death made him an object of veneration, the Fourth Gospel gives us nothing better than a lay-figure endowed with supernatural knowledge, but always the same, and devoid of living features--a figure which was only meant to serve the purpose of revealing Jesus majesty.

12. INJUDICIOUS RELIANCE ON THE SYNOPTICS.

How is it that the circumstances of many events are so obscurely sketched in the Fourth Gospel? We can some times explain this quite definitely. It is because the author starts in a careless way from an account in the Synoptics. Thus we had an instance (p. 51) already in vi. 3, 15, where Jesus twice ascends the mountain, without in the meantime having come down. This again explains a fact we noted as far back as p. 12, that in vi. 1, Jesus betakes himself to the other shore of the Lake of Galilee, whereas in the whole of the fifth chapter we have found him in Jerusalem. Without any further explanation, the Synoptics (Mk. vi. 32), and they alone, can represent him as crossing the Lake, because in the Synoptics he is always in Galilee; Jn. has carelessly followed them, without reflecting that he should have told us first how Jesus came from Jerusalem to Galilee--a matter which he reports quite appropriately in other places (iv. 3, 43).

But the most important example of his following the Synoptics and at the same time carelessly tacking his story on to theirs, is found in Jn.'s account (xii. 1-8) of the anointing of Jesus. Several striking features in it we have already noticed (p. 77 f .); we must now explain how these originated. Jn.

found an anointing of Jesus reported twice in the Synoptics j in Mk. (xiv. 3-9) and Mt. (xxvi. 6-13), one in Bethany near Jerusalem shortly before his death, in Lk. (vii. 36-50) one in Galilee, a long time before it. And yet in both cases the master of the house is called Simon. Moreover, in Mk. and Mt. he is (had been) a leper; in Lk. he is a Pharisee. But the fact that the names were alike seems to have been sufficient to lead Jn. to believe that in both cases the same event was intended. The woman therefore who anointed Jesus in this case must have been the same sinful woman who did so in Lk. (Mk. and Mt. tell us nothing beyond the fact that a woman anointed Jesus). But Jn. is prepared to say that it was that pious Mary who, according to the beautiful story in Lk. (x. 38-42), sat at Jesus' feet and listened to him, while her sister Martha busied herself more than was necessary with the household affairs. How did he obtain this knowledge? Not from Lk. , for in this Gospel the two sisters live in an unnamed village at which Jesus stops on his way through Samaria. We know already from xi. 1 f. that Jn. believed they lived in Bethany near Jerusalem and that Lazarus was their brother. Comparing the account of Lk., which Jn. drags in here, it suits the circumstances when at the meal Martha undertakes the serving and Mary anoints Jesus; this quite harmonizes with the fact that in Lk.'s Gospel she listens to him so attentively.

Must we indeed believe that all this was really observed by an eye-witness John? Or have events which, according to the Synoptics, happened at three different places with quite different persons and in a quite different way been simply worked up into one in the style of the writer of Jn.? That may be best decided by a consideration of the last fact which he reports: Mary anointed Jesus' feet and dried them with her hair. She could hardly have done anything more awkward. The ointment was too precious to be used for her hair. On this point Judas, who afterwards betrayed his Lord, was right; the ointment should have been sold and the proceeds (about 240 shillings) given to the poor (xii. 5). No; no such anointing was observed by any eye-witness; it owes its origin simply to a wrong use of the two accounts in Lk. There the sinful woman moistens Jesus' feet with her tears and then dries them with her hair; she anoints them afterwards, not before. But the tears of a sinful woman do not suit the case of Mary. Jn. therefore omits them. And, having done this, the anointing has to come first; otherwise there would be nothing to wipe away. We see then that there is really no reason to think the Synoptics wrong. We see also that Mary is not the woman who anointed Jesus' feet; the name of the woman will always be unknown to us. The same is true of the dwelling-place of Mary and Martha. That this was Bethany is a fact which existed only in the imagination of the Fourth Evangelist.

13. ASTOUNDING NATURE OF THE MIRACLES IN JN.

The raising of Lazarus, which is supposed to have taken place in Bethany, suggests that at this point it may be well to say all that remains to be said about the astounding nature of the miracles in the Fourth Gospel. What we shall say applies equally to the turning of water into wine at Cana, to the healing at the Pool of Bethesda of the man who had been lame for thirty-eight years, to the cure of the man born blind, &c. But it may suffice to explain what we mean, by dealing with the raising of Lazarus, which did not take place until the fourth day after death, when the body would already have become putrid. Martha actually refers to this fact (xi. 39), with the idea of suggesting that Jesus need not trouble to have the stone, which closed the rock-hewn selpulchre, rolled away. There is nothing which so clearly reveals the astounding nature of this miracle as the way in which it is regarded by scholars who assure us with the greatest earnestness that they do believe in miracles. They will tell us not only that the utterance of Martha is based upon a pure conjecture, but also that her conjecture was wrong. Certainly they can never have been inside a mortuary; nor do they reflect that in the warm climate of Palestine decomposition began much sooner than it does with us (cp. p. 19). Again they will tell us that, when a man dies, hearing is the last of all his senses to fail; and for this reason we are expressly told (xi. 43) that Jesus cried with a loud voice, "Lazarus, come forth." Indeed, they are able to tell us more. They will tell us that the bands in which, according to xi. 44, Lazarus' feet and hands were wrapped, were not fastened round his feet tightly. That Jesus could raise a man on the fourth day after his death they believe, and they expect every one who does not wish to be called an unbeliever to believe it too; but that he could give the man power to walk with firmly fastened feet--no, this they do not believe. Can we wonder then that other people refuse to accept as credible not only this narrative, but with it the whole book which produces it, and lays such emphasis on it, as principal evidence for the divine power of Jesus?

14. ARE MIRACLES POSSIBLE?

We ourselves do not at once assume this attitude, We remember not only that an incredible story may have found its way even into a book which is otherwise credible; we feel bound also to examine more closely the actual manner in which it is demonstrated that this miracle-story as well as the others in the Fourth Gospel and in the Bible generally do not deserve to be believed. In the last resort most people, we may be sure, rely in this matter on the idea that miracles are quite impossible. But the idea is not so firmly established as is commonly supposed. At the outset, it is certainly remarkable that it does not have the slightest influence on one who believes in miracles. Now we might say that the person who believes in miracles is unable to think correctly. But even his opponent will feel that his own case is not very strong when a miracle-story is brought to his notice which is attested by people who are worth considering, and when he has nothing better to say against it than, "Ah yes, but there are no such things as miracles," without being able to show, in this particular occurrence, how what seems miraculous in it can have arisen in a natural way. This reflection may lead us to what--regarding the matter from a strictly scientific standpoint--lies at the root of this question.

If we are to be able to say that a matter has been proved, it is necessary that it should have been proved by facts. In the case of a miracle-story, for example, we consider it to have been really proved that nothing miraculous happened, only when we have found the same phenomenon reappearing a second time and are certain that here no other than quite natural causes have operated. We call this kind of proof, proof from experience. The other kind is known as proof from reasoning. Whoever uses the latter in support of the contention that there are no miracles will say either, that the laws of Nature are unalterable, and a miracle would be no miracle unless one or more of the laws of nature were suspended; or he will say, it would be a contradiction of His character, rightly understood, if God were to suspend the laws of Nature the operation of which He has made so inviolable.

Let us devote just a few words to the notion--unfortunately very common among theologians--that a miracle is not contrary to the laws of Nature, but that certain forces come into operation which are quite natural but are not as yet known to us. Of course in earlier times Electricity and quite a short time ago the Röntgen rays were not known to us, and some occurrence due to these forces might easily have seemed miraculous, so that no man, even if he were only half-witted, would think of denying that all the forces of Nature are not as yet known to us. But what is the use of calling something a miracle which is due to forces like these which are quite natural, though still unknown to us? These are miracles which no one in the world would regard as impossible. But the chief aim of those who pride themselves on believing in miracles is to distinguish themselves in this way--to their own advantage--from those who do not believe in them and for this reason, in the opinion of their opponents, deserve to be called "infidels." That they have no right to make free with these quite natural but unknown forces, and by calling them to their aid to make miracles of as many occurrences as possible, is a fact that we need only mention in passing.

Another favourite contention is that in working a miracle God only makes certain forces, which are natural and known to us, operate in an extraordinary way, just as a man does when he makes a clock strike before the hour by moving the hand. We refrain from insisting here that such intervention on the part of God would involve a breach in the natural order of things, for this reflection will not trouble those who imagine the natural order of things to be not something unconditionally willed by God, a part of His own nature, but a limitation imposed upon him (by whom?), and who are only satisfied, nay can only see in Him a living God when (as happens rarely enough) He breaks through this limitation. But of course it is nothing better than a very naive presumption to suppose that a miracle which really deserves to be called one is prearranged by and adjusted to preconditions in exactly the same way as the premature striking of a clock. To produce bread for five thousand men--supposing that it were prearranged in some such way--flour, leaven, and heat must have been ready at hand. To increase the number of fish for the feeding, spawn and time for growth, or at least a good catch, and in any case heat, would again have been necessary; to walk upon the sea some quality in the water would have been needed to offer to the feet some power of resistance like that of a firm body; for a cure there must have been in the body a condition quite different from that which favours the continuance of sickness, though for the most part we cannot exactly define the condition necessary for disease or recovery. We must therefore disregard such statements, and reckon seriously with the fact that a miracle under all circumstances is a violation of the laws of Nature.

But if any one who for this reason pronounces miracles to be impossible is asked how he would prove it, he can in reality make no other reply than this: "I have come to that conclusion after using my reason to the best of my power." But this conclusion is not drawn by every one, whereas a fact of experience is recognised by all. And supposing he should say: "If the laws of Nature could ever cease to operate, there could no longer be any such study as Natural Science, we could no longer construct machines, and reckon on the working of a machine or of any other force in Nature"; the answer would be somewhat as follows: the point is not whether we can do all this, but how the world is actually constituted; if there are miracles in it, the fact is that we cannot do any of these things for certain.

Now it has been proved, and proved by experience, that we can do these things; and whenever things do not work as the natural scientist or the technical worker expected, he regularly finds out afterwards that the fault is not with Nature, but that he himself has made a miscalculation and been the cause of the failure. But, strictly speaking, what this means is only that the number of miracles, if miracles there are, must be very small, and moreover the fact only applies to the present time; as regards the distant past, before every occurrence was observed as closely as it is now, one may still suppose that miracles happened in greater number. To try to dispute this with any prospect of success, one should be able to investigate all the miracle-stories of the past which have come down to us, and to show the events to have been perfectly natural; but we are no longer in a position to do this. In fact, even if we were, it would not help us sufficiently; for miracles might have happened which have not been recorded at all. And were it possible to trace these also to natural causes, we should be powerless to prevent an event taking place to-morrow which we should be obliged to recognise as a miracle, and nothing would then be gained by the statement that there are no such things as miracles. A scientific caution therefore bids us in no case to make this statement a guiding principle.

15. MUST WE BELIEVE IN MIRACLES?

But we have only reached this result quite provisionally. It will take us a step further if I may be allowed to recall a personal experience. When I had occasion some years ago to express the above ideas to my class at the University, as they left the class-room they shook their heads and said, "He believes in miracles." I had certainly given them credit for more intelligence. To hold that it is not right to deny unconditionally that miracles are possible, and to believe that miracles do really happen, are two entirely different things. All that has been said so far only amounts to saying that in forming my opinion about miracles I must not be guided by general ideas, but by experience. But from experience I know for certain that I have never yet seen a miracle. I know also that pretty well all the miracles which are supposed to have happened in the present age have turned out, upon more careful inquiry, to be perfectly natural occurrences. I know too that the certainty with which the natural scientist and the technical worker reckon has never yet failed them. As regards the miracles of the past, I know that we can find no reason for supposing that miracles could have happened then more easily than to-day. In particular, I know that to say that God was obliged to use miracles for the purpose of proving Jesus to be the Saviour of the world is a bare assertion and cannot be proved. The Bible tells us that Paul, as well as Jesus, and very many ordinary persons in the Christian communities, and in fact--a still more important point--even the disciples of the Pharisees and other contemporaries of Jesus, possessed the power of working miracles (Rom. xv. 19; 2 Cor. xii. 12; 1 Cor. xii. 9 f., 28; Mt. xii. 27, vii. 22 f.; Mk. ix. 38-40); and yet none of these was ever regarded as the Saviour. Had Jesus worked ever so many miracles, without being at the same time a physician of souls, I know that he would not have been worshipped as the Saviour, and that we of to-day should not be called by his name.

And what is the use of the knowledge we possess of so many other religions if we refuse to use it in order to find out the origin of our own? Works of wonder are ascribed to every founder of a great religion of whose life we possess records, and they are often much more astounding than those attributed to Jesus; and--what is most remarkable here--in the case of each one of them utterances have at the same time been preserved in which he absolutely declines, as Jesus did (see above, p. 21 f.), to work miracles, and refers to them as matters of quite minor importance.

In the case of Buddha the utterance is preserved: "I do not teach my disciples, Do miracles by means of your supernatural power . . .; I say to them, Live by concealing your good works and making your sins to be seen." Confucius, the founder of the Chinese religion, or rather of their political and moral science, is reported to have said: "Investigate what is obscure, do what is wonderful, that later generations may say of it, I do not like these things." In the case of Zarathustra, the founder of the Persian religion as committed to writing in the Zend-Avesta, we read: "God said to me, If the king asks for a sign, do thou say, Only read the Zend-Avesta, and you will need no miracles." In the Koran we find God saying to Muhammed: "Thy destiny is to preach and not to do miracles." Muhammed appeals to God's great miracles, the rising and setting of the sun, the rain, the growth of the plants, and the birth of souls; these are the true wonders to those who know what faith is. [5] Very much that is told us about these founders of religion is untrustworthy. But these utterances deserve to be believed without question; for who could have invented them?

To these we may add in conclusion the saying of Kant, the founder of the newer philosophy: "Wise governments have at all times conceded, in fact have legally incorporated the notion in the public doctrines of religion, that in olden times miracles happened, but they have not allowed new miracles to happen. As regards new wonder-workers, they must have feared the effects they might have on the public peace and the established order." It is not difficult in the case of so clear a thinker to read between the lines: if, he would say, in olden times there had already been a wise government, it would not have allowed miracles to happen even in those days.

From which presupposition then ought we to start, if we wish to decide the question whether miracle-stories deserve belief? Strictly speaking, from none. But that is not possible. We always bring to the consideration of a subject some kind of presupposition. After what has been said, this must not be to the effect that miracles are not possible. But it would be still worse to assume, that miracles may easily happen. One who starts with this presupposition will certainly regard many occurrences as miracles in which everything has been brought about by causes which are quite natural. If then we cannot avoid starting with a presupposition, it can only of course be one that has already stood its trial in other cases, not one which has never yet been tested. In the present case therefore it can only be this, that any miracle-story we propose to examine will, presumably, admit of exactly the same natural explanation as others which we have so far been able closely to investigate. It is therefore not only permissible, but is our bounden duty, to try with all the means at our disposal to explain such matters by natural causes. While we do this, we must be ready to find a miracle if necessary, but only when there are insurmountable obstacles to our regarding a matter otherwise.

Until such obstacles arise, we are entitled to accept the two statements, (1) that the laws of Nature are unchangeable and (2) that God himself does not desire to suspend them by a miracle. Only we must be clear on this point--that they are not matters which have been proved quite sufficiently, but in spite of all that can be advanced in their favour, are never anything more than a belief.

If we know a miracle-story only from written accounts--which is the case with those of the Bible-- the first question we must ask is, Do these accounts show themselves to be reliable in every detail? For instance, it is not a matter of no importance, whether Jesus healed one blind man before he entered the city of Jericho (so Lk. xviii. 35-43) or healed him after he left it (so Mk. x. 46-52), or whether he healed two blind men (so Mt. xx. 29-34) at the same place. Why should I take it for granted that the Evangelists or their authorities duly informed them selves that it was really a case of blindness, when they are not agreed as to where and in the case of how many per sons the thing was done? Nor is it any more a matter of indifference whether on the evening after Jesus had healed Peter's wife's mother, people brought all the sick to him and he healed many of them (so Mk. i. 32-34), or whether they brought many and he healed all (so Mt. viii. 16), or whether they brought all and he healed them all (so Lk. iv. 40). Nor again is it a matter of no importance whether he taught the multitude before the Feeding of the Five Thousand (so Mk. vi. 34), or whether he healed their sick (so Mt. xiv. 14). We might continue thus for a long time if we wished /to throw light on this aspect of the miracle-stories found in the Synoptics. But the points we have mentioned are only intended to serve as examples of the kind of thing we are obliged to take note of in the stories of the Fourth Gospel.

16. SILENCE OP THE SYNOPTICS AS TO THE MIRACLES IN JN.

As compared with the stories in the Synoptics, the only one in Jn. that can be said to contain an actual contradiction is that of Jesus' walking on the sea, since Jesus crossed not merely a part but the whole of the sea, and is not supposed to have been taken into the boat (see above, p. 19 f.). In the other miracle stories in this Gospel (apart from that of the Feeding), contradictions are impossible, because the Synoptics do not include the stories. But this silence on their part is the very thing that cannot fail to make us feel the most serious doubts. These miracles which are known only to the Fourth Gospel are actually the most stupendous recorded: the turning of the water into wine at Cana, the healing of the man who was thirty-eight years a paralytic at the Pool of Bethesda, the cure of the man born blind, and the raising of Lazarus. (It is difficult to say whether by the cure of the son of a royal official at Capernaum, iv. 46-54, the same event is intended as the cure of the son or servant of the centurion at Capernaum in Mt. viii. 5-13 and Lk. vii., 1-10; see p. 99 f.)

Why these particular miracles should have been passed over by the Synoptics, if they really happened, it is absolutely impossible to imagine. What real arguments have those scholars who hold them to be true to offer, in order to explain the fact that there is not a word about them in the Synoptics? Once more it will be sufficient to fix our attention on the Raising of Lazarus.

We are told, for instance, that among the great mass of persons who were raised (!) by Jesus, the Synoptists might easily have forgotten Lazarus; or that they did not think themselves gifted enough to be able to gather up the preeminent importance of the event for the career of Jesus; or that they did not credit themselves with sufficiently delicate and lively feeling to be able to report it worthily; or that they were silent out of respect for the relatives of Lazarus who were still living (as if the story would not, on the contrary, have redounded to their honour); or that they did not think themselves to be sufficiently well instructed as to the details; or that the matter did not come to their ears because it took place before the arrival of the pilgrims from Galilee for the Easter festival (this would be to disregard xi. 16, where it is expressly said that all the twelve disciples of Jesus were present); or that it did not come to their ears because, when they arrived in Jerusalem, it was already too well known; or that the plan which they followed in their Gospels, apart from the last week of the life of Jesus, did not allow of their reporting events in Judaea. but only those which happened in Galilee; or that they were already aware that John, the beloved disciple of Jesus, would write his Gospel after them, and they wished to leave him to relate the Raising of Lazarus.

It could not really be shown in a more lamentable way that we cannot discover a single intelligible reason why the Synoptists have not related the Raising of Lazarus. To make such statements is at the same time to pronounce sentence that the event never happened. We see then that to arrive at this conviction it was not necessary to be shy of miracles; the way in which the story is told is in itself quite sufficient for our conclusion. And this is equally true of the other miracle stories which are found only in Jn.

17. THE MIRACLES IN JN. SYMBOLIC.

But why does Jn. introduce such incredible matters? Is it purely from a delight in the wonderful? Is it from the idea that Jesus could only in this way have shown himself to be the Saviour? Certainly he held this idea, and even attached importance to it (see p. 20 f.). But we should be doing him a great wrong, if we were disposed to think this his sole motive for telling us that such miracles were worked by Jesus. The fact that he describes so few in detail is itself an argument against this. But he also makes us realise clearly that each of these miracles has a deeper sense, a symbolic meaning; that is to say, that it is meant to express a religious idea in a picture as it were. In the case of the .Raising of Lazarus, he himself has supplied in the clearest manner the legend to the picture. Martha expresses to Jesus clearly, if shyly, her hope that he will raise her brother: "Lord, if thou hadst been here, my brother had not died. And even now I know that whatsoever thou shalt ask of God, God will give thee" (xi. 21 f.). Jesus answered, "Thy brother shall rise again." Martha rejoins, "I know that he shall rise again in the resurrection at the last day." And thereupon Jesus said to her, "I am the resurrection and the life: he that believeth on me, though he die, yet shall he live: and whosoever liveth and believeth on me shall never die." Here therefore we have the well-known and beautiful idea in the Fourth Gospel of that eternal life, in a deeply spiritual sense, which, through faith in Jesus, begins even during this earthly existence, and not merely after death, and which cannot be interrupted by the death of the body (cp. further especially v. 24).

Is it the same thing when Lazarus is immediately after wards summoned to come forth from the grave? By no means. Lazarus receives back the life of the body; but that spiritually eternal life of which we have spoken is a treasure which is stored in the depth of one's heart. To call Lazarus back to life, one of the greatest miraculous interventions in the laws of Nature was required; to bring to birth the spiritually eternal life of which we have spoken, only faith was needed. Lazarus can do nothing to help himself to come forth from the grave; whoever wishes to have the spiritually eternal life, must himself do his best within his own heart to call forth faith. Sooner or later Lazarus must die again; the spiritually eternal life, once gained, can never again be lost. Finally, Lazarus is only one man, and though we are certain that Jesus loved all other men, yet he is obliged to leave them all in the grave; but the spiritually eternal life is to be denied to no one. In brief, the thought of that eternal life which Jesus here speaks of as the essence of his message to Martha rises high as the heavens above the work which he afterwards per forms on Lazarus; so high that it has even been thought that the two things were not originally connected, and that the Raising of Lazarus was inserted in the original book of Jn. by a later writer. That is of course a great mistake. Both belong together very well, but only in the same way as a deeply spiritual thought belongs to the picture which gives it clear, if inadequate, expression in a visible occurrence.

Imagine a painter who wishes by means of his art to represent the thought: "Whosoever believes on me will live, even though he dies, and whosoever lives and believes on me will never die." Can he represent the feeling of his heart on canvas? What better symbol will he choose than the summoning of Lazarus, the friend of Jesus, from the grave? And is he obliged to make it real to our eyes in an obscure and indistinct way, because he does not suppose that the event really happened, but only wishes to awaken an idea in the soul of the beholder? We shall call him nothing better than a bungler, if he fails to represent, in a stirring way, how Jesus, while the onlookers are nervously expectant, stands in front of the sepulchre and cries out with arm upraised, "Lazarus, come forth," while behind the stone door, which has been rolled aside from the hollow vault, is seen the figure of the dead man wrapped in bands. And are we ready to reproach the author of the Fourth Gospel for using his art with equal vigour and effectiveness--the art of painting with words, instead of with the brush? Are we ready to reproach him, because we do not believe that what he paints on his canvas really happened, and because perhaps he also did not believe it?

Did he also not believe it? That would certainly be the most noteworthy aspect of the matter. Before we enter more closely into the question whether we ought to think this, we must take a wider survey. Clearly, the Raising of Lazarus is by no means the only instance in which a miracle is used to represent an idea. On the contrary, this point of view can be applied very easily to all the miracle-stories of the Fourth Gospel; and for the most part the Evangelist himself supplies us with a very clear clue. The legend which should be inscribed under the picture of the healing of the man born blind is found in viii. 12: "I am the light of the world: he that followeth me shall not walk in the darkness, but shall have the light of life" (cp. ix. 5, 39). The Feeding of the Five Thousand is explained in the discourses attached to it, vi. 26-35a, 36-51a, as a spiritual enjoyment of the person of Jesus, he being described as the true bread that comes from heaven: people must take his whole nature into themselves, or in other words, must believe in him (vi. 28 f.). At the same time the Feeding is here meant to represent the Supper; if this were not so, there could not be mention in vi. 51b-58 of the eating of Jesus flesh and at the same time of the drinking (cp. what is already said in vi. 35b) of his blood, not a word having been said in the Feeding of the Five Thousand to the effect that Jesus handed a cup to the disciples. Here indeed emerges the quite remarkable fact that Jesus, about the time of the second Passover feast, which occurred during his public ministry (vi. 4), gives his disciples an explanation of the meaning of the Supper, which, according to the same Gospel, he did not celebrate with them at all, and according to the Synoptics not until a year later; yet the discourses in chapter vi. do not permit of the least doubt that the Supper is really alluded to.

But if this is once assured, it is no longer difficult to recognise also the deeper meaning of Jesus' Walking on the Sea, which is linked to the Feeding of the Five Thousand as an event of the same evening. True, it might be thought that it has simply been taken over from the Synoptics, where also it follows the Feeding. But, as a matter of fact, Jn. does not repeat other miracle-stories found in the Synoptics. His repetition of this one, however, fits in very well with his purpose. When the Supper is celebrated at one and the same time in the most diverse places throughout the whole of Christendom, it is presupposed everywhere that Jesus is present at the celebration. Yet this could not be, if he were subject to the laws by which man is confined to the limits of space. Now, no single story in the Synoptics better expresses the idea that he was not so limited than that of the walking on the sea; consequently, it is certainly meant to serve to support the belief that at every celebration of the Supper Jesus is really near to his followers.

In the case of the sick man at the Pool of Bethesda we have a clue as to how we are to understand his sickness, as regards the time it had lasted. For thirty-eight years the people of Israel had been obliged, as a punishment for their disobedience to God, to wander in the wilderness, without being permitted to set foot on the promised land of Canaan (Deut. i. 34 f., ii. 14). The sick man thus represents the Jewish people, and in the five porticoes of the house in which he has so long hoped for a cure (Jn. v. 2) we may easily recognise the five books of Moses, obedience to which had been no help to the people. Jesus was the first to be able to bring to an end the period of their banishment from the land of peace and quiet; but since the people had opposed the will of God, he was obliged to say first, "Wilt thou be whole?" (v. 6).

The wine into which Jesus changed the water at Cana is then, of course, the new, glowing and inspiring religion which Jesus puts in the place of a weak Judaism. With this is grouped--and not without intention--the expulsion of the dealers and moneychangers from the fore-court of the Temple (ii. 1-11, 13-22). It was this act that showed most clearly how necessary it was to displace the old religion.

Again, with the healing at the Pool of Bethesda is connected that of the son of the royal official at Capernaum (iv. 46-54; v. 1-18). In order also to understand this miracle-story, the last that remains in Jn., we must take note of the points in which it differs from that concerning the Centurion at Capernaum in Mt. (viii. 5-13) and Lk. (vii. 1-10), a story which so manifestly lies at the root of it that perhaps the same event may be supposed to be intended in both cases. This centurion is a Gentile, who by his faith excels and puts the Jews to shame. In Jn., however, there appears in his place an officer of the king (so we read in Jn. as in Mk. vi. 14; Mt. xiv. 9 inexactly instead of "of the prince"; see Mt. xiv. 1; Lk. iii. 1, 19), Herod Antipas of Galilee, and we must take him to be a Jew, since, if he were not, the contrary would have been expressly stated. By his faith he also distinguishes himself, though not like the centurion by excelling all Jews, but only those who wish to see signs and wonders before they will believe in Jesus divine power. At first, no doubt in order to prove him, Jesus assumes that he shares the same disposition (iv. 48), but the man frees himself from this suspicion by taking Jesus at his word, when he says that he will make his son whole. We must, therefore, see in him a picture of that better section of the Jewish people which intercedes for the sick section; that is to say, for those who do not believe in Jesus. The latter is represented by the son of the official, just as in the other case it is by the sick man at Bethesda. Just because the sick man of the first story, like the sound official who makes petition for him, represents a section of the Jewish people, he must be described as his son and not as his servant, as in the case of the centurion of Capernaum according to Lk., and perhaps also according to Mt. Though the Greek word in Mt. (pais) may mean, not merely servant, but, equally well, son, and Jn. might keep this second meaning because it suited him better.

18. THE FEEDING A FACT FOR JN. IN SPITE OF ALL?

Thus in all the miracle-stories of the Fourth Gospel, a deeper thought can be recognised which they present vividly to us as in a picture. Now, as regards the problem suggested above (p. 97), when we were dealing with the Raising of Lazarus, whether in spite of all that has been said, the author held them to be actual occurrences, for the present this at least is clear, that the interest in the question whether a miracle really happened becomes secondary at once, if the miracle is used to represent nothing more than an idea. And so we discover in these stories some discord in the thought of the Fourth Evangelist. Side by side with the absolute value that he attaches to Jesus' works of wonder being recognised as real occurrences (p. 21), we note a certain indifference to the matter. Nor is it necessary to base this conclusion entirely upon our present examination; he has given even more definite expression to this indifference in other places. When many in Jerusalem believed on Jesus on account of his works of wonder, he did not trust himself unto them (ii. 23 f.), and Thomas, who would not believe on Jesus resurrection until lie had touched his wounds, was told, "Blessed are they that have not seen and yet have believed" (xx. 27-29). If we felt ourselves absolutely bound to go farther and to conjecture that Jn. first conceived his pictures in his own brain, just as a modern painter does, it would hardly be thinkable that afterwards he could have believed what he had depicted to be real events. What then is the truth?

Something more certain from which to start in this matter is found in the Synoptics. According to Mk. (viii. 14-21) the disciples, when they journeyed across the Lake of Galilee, had forgotten to take bread. Jesus then says to them: "Take heed, beware of the leaven of the Pharisees and the leaven of Herod" (or according to Mt. xvi. 6, "and the leaven of the Sadducees"). They imagine that he wishes to warn them against procuring loaves from the Pharisees and the others. Jesus notes this and says, "Do ye not perceive nor understand? . . . and do ye not remember? When I brake the five loaves among the five thousand, how many baskets (full of broken pieces) took ye up? . . . And when the seven among the four thousand, how many baskets took ye up?" (so according to Mt.). "Do ye not yet understand?" Mt. fittingly completes Jesus utterance thus: "that I spake not to you concerning bread? But beware of the leaven of the Pharisees and Sadducees. Then understood they how that he bade them not beware of the leaven of bread, but of the teaching of the Pharisees and Sadducees."

Shortly before, Mk. and Mt. have recounted the Feeding of the Five Thousand and that of the Four Thousand as actual occurrences. When Jesus now reminds the disciples of these, they must have been confirmed in their first thought, that by the leaven of which they were to beware he meant real loaves, and must have believed that, to make up for the omission, he would procure them loaves in as wonderful a way as he had done in the case of the two Feedings. Now, it would in itself be very surprising that Jesus should have offered to repair a piece of forgetfulness on the part of the disciples by exercising his miraculous power. In such a case, we certainly could not speak of a higher divine purpose for which he used this miraculous power, and say that he was actuated by love and compassion. But such reflections are not really necessary. The result of Jesus calling to mind the two Feedings is this: the disciples see that he does not wish to speak of loaves; and this is simply impossible. Have the Evangelists, then, told us something that is meaningless? That would be equally inconceivable. How can they have come to say the contrary of what is as clear as daylight?

The solution of the riddle is, however, not so difficult after all; we must only have the courage to think out the ideas of the story to the end. If the disciples by that of which Jesus reminds them are made to see that by leaven Jesus did not mean loaves but teaching, then in those earlier cases they cannot have seen and eaten loaves, but must simply have heard about loaves--and have heard too that the loaves meant teaching. In other words, the things of which they were reminded (and rightly reminded), when they thought of the Feedings, were not events in the life of Jesus, but discourses, in which he had compared his teaching with bread, by which the soul is satisfied. Now it suddenly dawns upon us also why more bread is said to have remained over than there was at first. Had the bread been real, this would have been a pure miracle. On the other hand, when Jesus propounds his teaching, it is quite natural that it should arouse new ideas in the minds of his hearers, and awaken new impulses; and that they them selves, enriching what they had heard by their own experiences and feelings, should carry it farther.

It is not enough, therefore, to see that the two miracle stories were certainly one at the beginning, and only came to be regarded as two distinct events at a later date when through the carelessness of the narrators the number of the partakers, of the loaves, and of the baskets of broken pieces, was changed. We must go farther and declare, in all seriousness, that no miraculous feeding took place, nor even a feeding which merely appeared miraculous. It would be tempting to us to explain the matter by sup posing that very many persons in the crowd were provided with more provisions than Jesus and his disciples, and that Jesus example simply induced them to place these at his disposal. But had this been the case, the disciples could just as little, by being reminded of it, have been led to understand that by leaven Jesus meant teaching, as they could by being reminded of a real miracle of feeding.

The only miraculous feature in the stories of the Feedings is therefore this: that by the side of them the story of the leaven of the Pharisees should also have found a place in the Gospels. Certainly Mk. and Mt. have not proved themselves very careful here; the words "Do ye not perceive?" apply to them also. But we have no reason to complain of them. If they had noticed the contradiction, they would certainly not have omitted the stories of the Feedings, but, rather, the narrative under consideration; and it would then have been much harder for us to recognise the real situation. In reality, they have faithfully preserved the narrative, because it had been transmitted to them. And we must recognise this with the greater satisfaction, because in other places in their Gospels we have been obliged to note many arbitrary alterations in the accounts, and because, again, it has not been possible for them to preserve correctly other matter, they themselves having become acquainted with it in a distorted form. Thus, for example, exactly what was narrated about Jesus' discourse concerning that remarkable bread (the teaching) which, when it was divided and partaken of, did not decrease but increased, will certainly at a very early date have been misunderstood by people who were not present, just as the Synoptists have misunderstood it, by including it in their books as a miraculous event.

How does what has been said help us to answer the question, In spite of the fact that to Jn. the Feeding was in part a representation of the spiritual appropriation of the nature of Jesus, and in part a representation of the Supper, did he regard it as a real event? In any case, we know at least that if he did so, he was wrong. But since there was a time when it was known that it was not a real event, it is not altogether inconceivable that Jn. too derived this knowledge from that time. On the other hand, this again is hardly likely, for the Synoptists themselves no longer possessed the knowledge, and Jn. did not write until after them and drew upon them. Such reflections therefore will hardly clear up our question. Nor is there any other way of fathoming the inmost thought of the Fourth Evangelist: and if we could dig deeper perhaps we might not find harmony and clearness, but simply a struggle between two points of view, the literal and the purely figurative.

But it is quite sufficient that to Jn. the story of the Feeding, regarded from one of these two points of view, serves merely to represent something spiritual. In this way he has in fact approached quite near, though perhaps in a very roundabout way (if he regards the Feeding as an actual event), to what we know from the Synoptists to have been the most original version--namely, that Jesus himself referred to the Feeding with bread simply as a figure-of-speech for the satisfaction of the soul by his teaching. The point of view in Jn. does not, it is true, agree with this quite exactly; but very much is gained already when we find him attaching no decisive value to the miracle as such. And the relatively slight divergence from the ideas of Jesus is at the same time characteristic of the general spirit of the Fourth Gospel. What, in Jesus' opinion, is offered to men to satisfy their souls is his teaching; what is offered them in Jn. is his person. To Jn. everything centres round his person; and even when he finds the Supper represented in the story of the Feeding, he imagines that when it is celebrated, it is the person of Jesus that in some mysterious way the partaker receives into himself.

19. ARE THE OTHER MIRACLES FACTS FOR JN.?

We must quote yet another passage from the Synoptics to elucidate the question as to what opinion the Fourth Evangelist held with regard to the miracle-stories. When John the Baptist was in prison, he sent his disciples to Jesus to ask whether he was the promised Saviour, or whether they must look for another. We must remember here that, from the time of the baptism of Jesus, John could not have been clear on this matter (see p. 79 f.). The answer of Jesus is almost verbally identical in Mt. (xi. 4-6) and in Lk. (vii. 22 f.): "Go your way and tell John the things which ye do hear and see: the blind receive their sight and the lame walk, the lepers are cleansed and the deaf hear, and the dead are raised up and the poor have good tidings preached to them. And blessed is he whosoever shall find none occasion of stumbling in me." Could Jesus have done anything more calculated to destroy the effect of his words than, in his list of works of wonder which reaches a climax in the awakening from the dead, to specify at the end of them preaching to the poor, that is to say, something quite ordinary, something not at all wonderful, something which could not make the slightest impression on the disciples of John as an answer to their question whether he was the promised Saviour, their ideas of his superhuman power being what they were. Or may we suppose that the Evangelists have inappropriately added this from clumsiness? Assuredly not. They have taken the greatest possible care that we should read in their books of all the five classes of wonders which Jesus enumerates before this answer to the Baptist.

Now, in both consistently (Mk. omits the whole story of the Baptist's messengers) there appear before this date only the healing of a leper (Mt. viii. 1-4 = Lk, v. 12-14) and of palsied men (Mt. viii. 5-13 = Lk. vii. 1-10; Mt. ix. l-8 = Lk. v. 17-26); and in Mt. (ix. 18-26), besides these, in agreement with the order of events in Mk. (v. 21-43), the awakening of the daughter of Jairus. This Lk. introduces too late for the answer to the Baptist's question (not until viii. 40-56). But, instead of it he has introduced earlier (vii. 11-17) the awakening of the young man at Nain, about which Mt. and even Mk. say nothing at all. On the other hand, Mt. ix. 27-34 introduces the healing of two blind men and a dumb man, about which Lk. and even Mk. are silent. In Jesus enumeration there is no dumb man, but mention is made of the deaf; since, however, both are described by the same Greek word (kophós), there do, as a matter of fact, appear in Mt. before chapter xi. all the ailments mentioned by Jesus. In Lk. the blind and the deaf are omitted. Instead of this, Lk. tells us in vii. 21 that in the presence of the messengers of the Baptist Jesus healed many blind and other ailing persons, about whom there is not a word in Mt.

Both Evangelists, therefore, although in complete disagreement with each other, have been at pains to make Jesus enumeration appear literally true; and, this being so, could they have deprived it of its whole force by making so unsuitable an addition (concerning the preaching to the poor)? Or was it perhaps later copyists who did this? But even in their case, the matter would be equally inexplicable.

There is here again, as in the question of Jesus utterance about leaven, only one solution: the most striking and seemingly the most embarrassing version must be the most original. Jesus himself must have added, "and the poor have the gospel preached to them." But he could only have done so if all the previously mentioned persons are on the same level, that is to say, if he meant spiritually blind, spiritually lame, spiritually leprous, spiritually deaf, and spiritually dead. And here again, just as in the case of the stories of feeding, the concluding words are intelligible only on this understanding. "Blessed is he whosoever finds none occasion of stumbling in me": this means that the Baptist should not take offence at Jesus for coming forward in such simple guise, as a mere teacher and prophet, and should recognise him as the promised Saviour, in spite of his humble appearance. This, in truth, was why John had had doubts on the matter. In thinking of the promised Messiah, he thought, as his whole race did, of a person who would come forward with superhuman power, drive the Romans from the land and set up a mighty kingdom, in which the Jews would reign.

Here then we have a new instance how utterances of Jesus have often been faithfully preserved in the Synoptics. In this saying we may depend upon it that we have the words of Jesus in all essentials, particularly in their conclusion, just as he spoke them (the question whether he enumerated at the beginning one ailment more or less need not detain us); and this is the more noteworthy, since the Evangelists have entirely misunderstood it, and have made great efforts to show that their misunderstanding is right. At the same time, we have in it a new example of the way in which Jesus availed himself of figurative language which might easily be misunderstood, and which actually was understood in such a manner that objective works of wonder were supposed to be intended when he had spoken merely of spiritual experiences unaccompanied by any miracle.

For the Fourth Gospel, therefore, we have here a foundation upon which to build if we would assume that not only the feeding of the five thousand, but also the healing of the man born blind, of the man paralysed for thirty-eight years, of the son of the royal official, and the awakening of Lazarus, were from the first meant to describe merely the healing of souls. It makes no difference, of course, if the son of the royal official is described as suffering, not from one of the ailments enumerated in Mt. xi. 5, but from a fever. In fact, by recognising this figurative style of speech, we may also venture to seek such an explanation of the last remaining miracles of the Fourth Gospel, the turning of water into wine at Cana, and Jesus' walking on the sea, even though these are not miracles of healing.

We may not, of course, in any case go as far as to sup pose that all these stories, in their figurative meaning, actually came from Jesus himself. Had they done so it would be inconceivable that about most of them the Synoptics should know nothing. What we gather, therefore, is at most this, that the author of the Fourth Gospel still had correct information as to the metaphorical style in which Jesus delighted to express himself, and that he copied this in the spirit of his master. At the same time, it is true, we must reckon fully with the possibility that he did not gain this by first-hand knowledge of Jesus style of speech, but in the roundabout way described above: he believed that in all his miracle-stories he had to do with real events; not until later did they become to him figures for mere ideas, and the question whether they really happened become of but secondary importance. Not even now are we able to come to a decision upon these two points of view; perhaps indeed, as already intimated, Jn. could not himself have said which of them he had finally adopted.

20. TRADITIONS KNOWN ONLY TO JN.?

In any case we must be quite clear that at the root of each of the two points of view there are quite distinct presuppositions. If Jn. from the first gave forth his miracle-stories merely as the figurative clothing of religious ideas, then we may be all the more certain that he invented them himself; he could not have had them from the lips of Jesus, for had that been their source the Synoptics also would have given them. If, on the other hand, Jn. regarded them as real events, then they must have come to him from some authorities in whom he had confidence. Is it possible perhaps to decide now which of the two suppositions is right? In other words, is there a tradition concerning the Life of Jesus which was known only to Jn. and remained unknown to the Synoptics?

The far-reaching importance of this question can be realised at once. If Jn. was acquainted with such a tradition, he may have derived from it all that he has in addition to what the Synoptics tell us; and in this much else is included besides the miracle narratives we have been considering. On this basis very many people immediately think they may assume that all these additional matters are also historical. But the pleasure which they thus give themselves is premature. Supposing that Jn. drew from a tradition--for the time being we are willing to assume that he did--have we then disposed of the question, Why do the Synoptics know nothing about this tradition? Who was the first to know of it? Was it the Apostle John? Could he really, in Jesus' lifetime, have noted certain things of which Peter and the other apostles had no experience? And yet the Synoptists themselves drew from the communications of the Apostles or of their disciples! We might acquiesce, if the things which appear only in the Fourth Gospel were all minor matters, In that case, we might think that to the other Apostles or to the Synoptics they seemed to be unimportant. But the healing of the man born blind, the healing of the man palsied for thirty-eight years, the raising of Lazarus, the farewell discourses of Jesus, the washing of the disciples' feet on the last evening of his life, etc.!

Or can we believe that some worshipper of Jesus--not further known to us--outside the circle of his twelve apostles, observed all these things, one, for instance, as people of late have been fond of suggesting, who lived in Judaea, and, having nothing to tell us about Galilee, had all the more to tell us about what Jesus did in Judaea? Of such an one it would be equally true to say that he could have observed nothing which the apostles did not also know of. Does not the Fourth Gospel say continually that they were all present on all these occasions?

It is thus, besides, quite immaterial whether we assume the eye-witness in question (whether we think of him as the apostle John or as one who was not an apostle) to have written the Fourth Gospel himself or only to have given information to the author. In no case can what this person alone tells us be derived from actual observation of the events; for, if it were, we should read of it in the Synoptics as well.

It may, nevertheless, have come to the Fourth Evangelist by tradition. The idea that a tradition must in all circumstances be correct is a very curious one. He to whom it is delivered may hold it to be correct; but before it reached him an error may have crept in. In view of what has been said, only on this presupposition is it worth while to speak of a tradition known only to the Fourth Evangelist. If we call it a "Johannine tradition," we must not be understood to mean that it started from the apostle John, but simply that it came by tradition to the Fourth Evangelist whom we, depending again upon a tradition, call John.

21. AMPLIFICATION OF THE STORY OF LAZARUS ON THE BASIS OF LK.

But instead of instituting general inquiries into such a tradition, we will at once show by examples how we may very easily think of the matter. We do not by any means assert that it must really have so happened; it is quite sufficient if it may have so happened. We will start again with the most instructive story in the Fourth Gospel, that of the Raising of Lazarus. His name reminds us of the parable in Lk. (xvi. 19-31), in which a Lazarus appears by the side of a rich man. At first sight the two narratives seem to be radically different: in Lk. we have before us a figure in a parable, in Jn. a real person; in Lk. a poor and sick man who after his death is compensated for his sufferings, in Jn. a man for whom neither sufferings nor compensation come in question. But the two figures have at any rate one point of contact. The rich man in Lk. (xvi. 27-31) in his torment wishes Abraham to send Lazarus back to earth to warn the brethren of the rich man. Abraham answers, "they have Moses and the prophets; let them hear them." The rich man objects: "Nay, father Abraham, but if one go to them from the dead, they will repent." Abraham, however, decides that "if they hear not Moses and the prophets, neither will they be persuaded if one rise from the dead."

Let us now imagine this parable to have been discussed in a sermon. It is not difficult to conjecture what may have been said. The brothers of the rich man who have Moses and the prophets are, of course, the Jews. The preacher had thus a most excellent opportunity of proving the truth of Abraham's concluding words, to the effect that even one who had risen from the dead would not induce them to repent. Jesus had actually risen, and, notwithstanding, the Jews, with trifling exceptions, had rejected his preaching, though so many heathen had accepted it. Now if Lazarus, in answer to the request of the rich man, had been sent back to earth to preach to his brethren, he would have been made to do in the parable what, according to the belief of Christians, Jesus in reality did by his resurrection. If the preacher reckoned on his hearers possessing some intelligence, he may perhaps, with raised finger, have continued the parable thus: "as a matter of fact, Lazarus has risen, and the brethren of the rich man have not listened to him." Some hearer who had not understood the delicate meaning of this turn it may even have been a woman hearer--then went home, we may further imagine, and said: "To-day the preacher said that Lazarus has arisen." "Really, such a thing I have never heard." "But he said so without a doubt." "Who awakened him then?" "He did not say that. But who should have awakened him, if it was not Jesus himself?"

In this way the kernel of the narrative in Jn. was provided: Lazarus has been awakened by Jesus. And without any idea of deception or forgery, without even any censurable indulgence in phantasies, but purely from a very excusable misunderstanding! We need not go on describing further how one little feature after another may have, now and again, been added. Let it suffice that this may very well have happened; and again without any idea of deception, but purely with the idea that the thing cannot well have happened in any other way. For instance, what was more natural than that Lazarus, before his death, should have been ill, and that Jesus should have been informed of this? If we only imagine a sufficient number of people contributing to the story, and adding one detail after another, the Fourth Evangelist in the end need only have dotted the i's, so to say, in order to get the story in due form into his book.

This consideration is by no means unimportant. It relieves him of the charge of having himself invented the whole narrative. Certainly we could not shrink from making this charge, if the attempt we have made above, to explain the matter differently, might not be considered successful; for the fact that Lazarus was not awakened, we do not now, after all that has been said, need to prove. In fact, we should have to ask ourselves whether this reproach of having invented the whole narrative would really be a reproach, since quite certainly we could not reproach the preacher in question with it, if, relying on the intelligence of his hearers, he carried the parable of Lk. a step further and said, Lazarus has arisen. But we have preferred our own theory because it has enabled us to assume that the raising of Lazarus was "delivered" to the Fourth Evangelist as a real miracle, and because we can understand better how, at least in many passages of his book, he could attach so much importance to the fact of this and the other miracles having really happened (p. 20 f.).

22. OTHER AMPLIFICATIONS IN JN.

Taking next the narrative of the healing of the man born blind, its origin could easily be understood on the sup position that some preacher discussed a story of the healing of another blind man taken from the Synoptics, and held the Jewish people to be meant by the man. In that case, it was very natural for him to say that this blind man was so from his birth. In a quite similar way, indeed, the discourse of Stephen (Acts vii.) aims at showing that the Jewish people had mistaken the will of God from the first. Some hearer who was not too attentive might easily have gathered from the discourse that Jesus had really healed a man who was blind from birth. In this particular case, however, we are in a position to say further how some of the details in the narrative in Jn. may have arisen. In Mk. viii. 22-25 we read that a blind man was made to see by Jesus, not at once but by degrees. If a preacher enlarged upon this, he might easily reach the thought: the spiritually blind only succeed gradually in recognising Jesus, the person who makes them whole. The thought is in Jn. ix. 17, 31-33, 38 expressed in such a way that the healed man at first regards Jesus only as a prophet and a devout man sent by God, and only in the end comes to perceive that he is the Son of man, in other words, the Saviour of the world. Further, from the same passage in Mk. the point in Jn. ix. 6 is borrowed, that Jesus' spittle served as the remedy. The only new features are the way in which this is used, and the washing of the eyes in the Pool of Shiloah.

For the story of the marriage-feast at Cana also (ii. 1-11) there were starting-points in the New Testament. In the future kingdom of eternal happiness people drink wine (Mk. xiv. 25). Figuratively, the new religion which Jesus introduces has already (in Mk. ii. 22) been compared with new wine which ought not to be poured into old skins; and the time during which Jesus is with his friends, whether in the present or in the future, is here (Mk. ii. 19) and elsewhere (Rev. xix. 7; Jn. iii. 29) described as a marriage festival. If we may believe that the Fourth Evangelist built his narrative upon these foundation stones, some one who was familiar with the figurative style of speech, or a number of such people, before Jn. may easily have done the same; and in that case the whole account would have been handed on to Jn. as a real miracle.

The origin of the story of the healing at the Pool of Bethesda we may suppose to have been rather different (v. 1-16). Here a preacher may not have started with some parable which had been handed down as coming from the mouth of Jesus. But he might certainly have taken the story in the Old Testament (Deut. ii. 14) as his starting-point, according to which the people of Israel, in punishment of its disobedience, was obliged to wander in the wilderness for thirty-eight years. Thus, in a figurative discourse, having in view all the while the people's whole history down to his own time, he might have described the nation as a sick person, who for thirty-eight years had been bed-ridden. Five porticoes--thus he went on per haps to recall the five books of Moses, by obedience to which the Jews hoped to be made blessed--had the house in which he lay, but he did not become well; often as the water was stirred, which held out to him the hope of a cure, there was never any one there to help him to step in, until Jesus came and asked him, Wilt thou be whole?

In this way the explanation may be applied to all the miracle-stories in Jn. which have not been taken directly from the Synoptics, like the feeding of the multitudes and the walking on the sea. Of other narratives, it perhaps suits best that of the washing of the disciples' feet. According to Lk. xxii. 26 f., immediately after the last occasion in his life on which he supped with his disciples, Jesus said, "I am in the midst of you as one that serveth." Now, washing the feet was one of the duties of the humblest servants. It may perhaps seem to us rather bold, but it is not unthinkable, that a preacher, wishing to describe very vividly Jesus condescension in serving his followers, may perhaps have said: "Jesus ministered to his disciples like the humblest slave; he compared himself with the servant who washes the feet of the guests at meal-time." Of course, he meant this only as a figure of speech; but it is very conceivable that it was understood as a real event which actually happened on the last evening of Jesus' life.

But enough. We do not press the application of this method of explanation to other accounts in the Fourth Gospel; for we by no means wish to derive all accounts not included in the Synoptics from a "tradition" only known to Jn., but only those in which this can be done naturally; and so we leave every reader to judge in how many cases the method is appropriate.

23. DIVERGENCE AS TO JESUS DEATH.

We must look all the more closely now into the one, but very important, point in which, with much plausibility, people may find in Jn. a correct tradition based upon faithful recollection, a tradition by which the story of the Synoptics is shown to be faulty. It concerns the day of Jesus' death. According to all four Gospels, Jesus died on a Friday. This was, according to the Synoptics (Mk. xiv. 12, 14; xv. 1), the 15th of the month Nisan (corresponding almost to our April), but according to Jn. (xiii. 1, 29; xviii. 28; xix. 14, 31) the 14th. This means an extremely serious difference. On the afternoon of the 14th Nisan the lambs were slain in the fore-court of the Temple at Jerusalem, and then after sunset, at the meal of the Passover festival (the place of which is taken by our Easter festival), were eaten. The 15th Nisan was the first of the seven days of the festival, and in sanctity and the strictness with which all work was refrained from, was almost equivalent to a Sabbath. It is important to remember that this is true also of the night between the 14th and the 15th of Nisan, because amongst the Jews the day began with sunset.

The difference between Jn. and the other Gospels is seen, therefore, particularly in two points. According to the Synoptics, Jesus celebrated the Passover meal, together with his disciples, on his last evening. But not according to Jn.; according to his account, Jesus' last supper was, rather, on the preceding day, which was not a feast-day; and when the Jews ate the Paschal lamb twenty-four hours later, he already lay in the grave. Consequently his arrest, condemnation, crucifixion, and burial, which according to both accounts were compressed into less than twenty-four hours (to the next sunset after his last supper), also followed, according to Jn., on the working-day before the festival; but according to the Synoptics on the first feast day which involved strict suspension of all work.

The following table will serve to make this clear. The days of the month Nisan, placed in the middle, are common to the Synoptics and Jn. The denotes the crucifixion of Jesus.

SYNOPTICS. JOHN. Wednesday. 13 Thursday. Thursday. 14
Evening Passover meal. Friday. Friday. 15 (1st feast-day). Saturday.

24. DAY OF JESUS DEATH ACCORDING TO THE SYNOPTICS CONCEIVABLE.

Was Jesus trial possible on the feast-day? It would seem not. And if Jn. is right, this point is so decisive that we may seek the truth in this Gospel everywhere else as well. He would, in that case, appear as the eye-witness whose purpose in his story is tacitly to correct the Synoptics (see above, pp. 52-57).

But consider what this means. Hitherto, as compared with the Synoptics, the Fourth Gospel has always proved less correct, and often quite untrustworthy. Is this discovery to be all at once reversed? May we believe that the Synoptists have made a mistake like this even on this one point (the day of Jesus' death)? Can we, if we do so, believe anything else at all in their books on any one point? What took place in these last hours of the life of Jesus must have stamped itself indelibly on the minds of the disciples. How could they have told, or merely through an obscure recital have suggested to their hearers, that their Lord was present to partake with them of the Jewish paschal meal, if this was not the case at all? How can they have wrongly stated, or only suggested, that he was arrested, condemned, crucified, and buried on the feast-day, when all this seems to be made impossible by the sanctity of the day itself? Of course, up to the present it seems an equally great riddle that Jn. should have been led by some mistake to relate the contrary. But, in any case, we have the most .pressing occasion to see exactly whether the statement of the Synoptics is really unacceptable.

According to Jewish law, as committed to writing in the Mishnah, the oldest part of the Talmud, about 200 A.D., in order to pass a death sentence two sittings of the High Council--that is to say, of the highest judicial court--were necessary, and a night must intervene between them. Now, since no judicial proceedings might be held on the Sabbath, a trial which might end in a death-sentence could not commence on the day before (and therefore also, we may be sure, on the day before the first day of the Feast of the Passover). On this view of the matter, the story of the Synoptics seems in all circumstances to be excluded; for, according to this, the first sitting took place in the night which to the Jews already formed part of the feast-day, and the second actually on the morning of this first feast-day (Mk. xiv. 17, 53-64; xv. 1). But--and this is a point which is not usually noted--even the Johannine account would be impossible. Even if we assume that a trial of Jesus took place in the palace of Caiaphas (xviii. 24-28), as it had already done (xviii. 13-23) in the palace of Annas (Jn. does not tell us at all what happened before Caiaphas), we must still insist that between the two trials there intervened not a night, but only a few hours of one and the same night. If in conformity with the regulations a night was to be allowed to intervene between the two sittings, the trial, even according to Jn., could not have commenced; for, according to his account, the 14th of Nisan had already begun when Jesus was arrested, so that the second trial could not have fallen before the 15th Nisan, which would mean the great feast-day.

Accordingly, as regards both stories, we cannot avoid devoting space to the following consideration.

At this time the Jews were no longer allowed to execute a sentence of death; that could be done only by the Roman governor, and so at that time by Pontius Pilate, who was present in Jerusalem throughout the Passover feast with a force of soldiers which had been increased on account of the immense throng of people. But, this being so, it was of no importance to the Jews to pass the death-sentence formally, since they had to ask Pilate to confirm and execute it. They could achieve their purpose equally well by simply making their charge against Jesus before Pilate without previously condemning him. The high-priest, who always presided, required in the first instance, therefore, simply to declare that no judicial court would be held, but only a charge be prepared to bring before Pilate; in that case, the law we have mentioned would have proved no obstacle. We may well believe that the High Council had shrewdness enough to hit upon this expedient.

Only consider, as regards the whole subject, how urgent the matter was! If, during the festival, the people were to declare for Jesus, recognising him as the Messiah, towards which recognition they had a few days before at Jesus entry into Jerusalem already made a very suspicious beginning (Mk. xi. 1-11), it would be too late to take action. The original determination to remove him had been formed even before the beginning of the festival (Mk. xiv. 1 f.). After the festival had started and Jesus had been arrested, not another hour was to be lost. The Christians heard nothing at all of that purely juristic observation of the high-priest, which we have conjectured; or they paid no attention to it for they saw in it, unquestionably and quite correctly, a mere excuse, and they held fast, in a way that we can very easily understand, to the familiar idea that the High Council was the highest judicial Court in their nation.

Simon, who was compelled to bear Jesus cross, was coming at the time "from the country" (Mk. xv. 21). But who can say that he had been working there? He belonged, in truth, to Cyrene in North Africa, and therefore clearly was one of the number of pilgrims who had come to Jerusalem solely in order to keep the feast. At such a feast two million men may easily have assembled; for we know that about 65 A.D. 256,500 paschal lambs were counted at the slaughter in the fore-court of the Temple, and no part of their flesh might be left over until the next morning (Ex. xii. 4, 10). Beyond question very many of those who had come to the feast must have passed the night outside the city, so that Simon may very well have returned to it before nine o'clock in the morning (Mk. xv. 25). The Greek words may mean not only "from the field," but equally well "from the country."

Similarly, from the fact that the Synoptics call the day of Jesus' death "the day of preparation" we may not conclude that they support Jn. when he tells us in his gospel that it was a working-day. "Day of preparation," that is to say, day for making preparations, was in fact the name of every Friday, because people prepared for the Sabbath by doing the works which were forbidden on the Sabbath itself. And this would be equally appropriate if the Friday were a feast-day; for some kinds of activity forbidden on the Sabbath were allowed then, particularly (see Ex. xii. 16) the cooking of foods, which were kept warm from every Friday evening to be used on the Sabbath when there could be no fire. Mk. expressly says (Mk. xv. 42) that the day of preparation was "the day before the Sabbath"; cp. Lk. xxiii. 54; Mt. xxvii. 62.

Jesus execution would not have been possible on the feast-day if the Jews themselves had had to carry it out. But as a matter of fact this was the business of Pilate; and what he did the Jewish authorities would not of course regard as a violation of the feast-day for which they could be held responsible. Nor was there any need to fear a rising among the people in favour of Jesus after Pilate had pronounced his sentence; it might be taken for granted that he would suppress anything of the kind with the utmost rigour.

Still less does the burial of Jesus, which according to all four Gospels (Mk. xv. 42-46; Jn. xix. 38-42) was carried out before sunset on the very day of Jesus' death, prove that the first feast-day had not begun before this sunset, as Jn. would have us believe (according to the Jewish division of the day). All four accounts agree that Jesus died on a Friday. If then the time of burial had been delayed because this (according to the Synoptics) was a feast-day, it would have fallen on a Sabbath, a day on which it must have been still more strictly excluded. Moreover, the burial on the day of death itself is not merely a custom (see above, p. 19), but in the case of one who has been hanged, is expressly commanded in the Law (Deut. xxi. 22 f.).

It was really forbidden in the Law (Exod. xii. 22) to leave the house in which the Passover meal had been eaten before the next morning. But this prohibition in view of the multitude of pilgrims, to which we have referred above, could certainly at this time no longer be obeyed. Even the custom enjoined in the same verse as well as in verse seven, of smearing the door-posts with the blood of the paschal lamb, was dispensed with. It seemed helpful to suppose that the practice had been ordained solely for the first celebration of the Passover before the Exodus from Egypt, and not for its later repetition (see v. 12 f.), though, as a matter of fact, in vv. 24 f. it is ordained "for ever." Jesus therefore may very well have gone to the Garden of Gethsemane with his disciples on the night which was included in the feast-day.

So far then we have not discovered a single point in which anything that the Synoptics tell us would have been really impossible on the feast-day to which they refer it. The case seems to be different when we read in Lk. (xxiii. 56) that the women prepared ointments, and in Mk. (xv. 46) that Joseph of

Arimathea bought a linen cloth in which to wrap the body of Jesus. True, we do not know whether these two things would be as strictly forbidden on such a feast-day as they were on the Sabbath. But if they were, the further question must always arise, Were the Synoptics really guilty of the great mistake of placing Jesus' death on a wrong day, or only of the small slip of recording on a side-issue something which the sanctity of the day made impossible? Would it not be quite excusable if they have pictured to themselves in a way that is not quite correct a matter which they did not witness themselves, and if they did so through not having a very accurate knowledge of Jewish regulations? Moreover, Mk. (xvi. 1), at any rate, says, in conformity with these, that the women did not buy the ointments until the Sabbath was over.

Similarly, the Synoptics may have been led astray by a pardonable error, when they suppose that the band of men sent by the Jewish authorities to capture Jesus were armed with swords (Mk. xiv. 43, 48). To carry a sword on the Sabbath, and therefore probably also on the night which, according to the Synoptics, was part of the feast-day, was forbidden. But this at any rate is certain, that the use of police on days when there was an immense throng of people could in no case be rendered impossible by a command which prohibited the carrying of any weapon. In the Mishnah, in fact, only the following weapons are for bidden; cuirasses, helmets, greaves, swords, bows, shields, slings (?), and spears. We may well believe that the Jews were sharp-witted enough to hit upon something which could not be included amongst these, and yet was a weapon all the same. Perhaps the Synoptics give us a real clue here, when they say that those who were sent by the Jewish authorities were armed with staves as well as with swords.

There is no reason to doubt that Jesus disciples had swords with them (Mk. xiv. 47). But they had themselves long given up the habit of painfully adhering to commands about such things as these. They had, of course, armed themselves on the preceding working-days, in order to be prepared against a sudden attack; and certainly on the night when they were exposed to greatest danger they would not have laid aside their swords, even though, strictly speaking, they were forbidden to carry them on the feast-day.

Let us draw the conclusion! Apart from unimportant side-issues, in which we can easily believe that mistakes may have been made, the Synoptists tell us nothing that might not have happened on the feast-day. The account in Jn., according to which the whole thing took place on a working-day is, it is true, easier to understand, but it does not by any means provide the only explanation. And it cannot surely be postulated that an event must have transpired in a way that can be understood easily. If that were so, how many events would have to be struck out of the pages of history! It is not necessary to reject an account, unless it is thoroughly inconceivable. But, as we have shown, that is by no means the case with that of the Synoptics. Consequently, we are fully justified in accepting it, seeing that on other points we have always been able to give more credit to the Synoptics than to Jn.

25. THE DAY OF JESUS DEATH ARTIFICIALLY FIXED IN JN.

True, it always remains a riddle how Jn. can have been led to give us his account, which, in view of what we have said, is necessarily wrong. But the riddle can be solved, and even Jn. himself expressly indicates how this may be done. According to xix. 31-36, Pilate, at the instigation of the Jews, gives command for the thighs of Jesus and of the two men who were crucified with him to be broken, that their death might be hastened, and that they might be buried before the sunset with which in Jn. the feast begins. But the soldiers find Jesus already dead, and therefore in his case do not carry out the command. Jn. then tells us that this happened in order that the passage in the Old Testament might be fulfilled: "a bone of him shall not be broken." Of whom? The paschal lamb (Ex. xii. 46). Consequently, Jn. regards Jesus as the true paschal lamb, and thinks that in him what is said of the paschal lamb in the Old Testament must be fulfilled. Paul had expressed the thought: "for our passover also hath been sacrificed, even Christ" (1 Cor. v. 7); Jn. elaborates it more exactly, and tells of the sufferings and death of Jesus as they must have happened if they were in precise agreement with the injunctions about the paschal lamb.

He does this, it should be noted, not merely in the matter we have mentioned, where he tells us that Jesus bones were not broken, but in every case where there are injunctions in the Old Testament about the lamb which might have been fulfilled in Jesus as well. The lamb had to be slain in the afternoon (Ex. xii. 6; Deut. xvi. 6: towards evening, but in Jesus time as early as from one or two o'clock). In accordance with this, Jesus is still standing before Pilate (Jn. xix. 14) at midday, though, according to the Synoptics (Mk. xv. 25), he was crucified at nine o'clock in the morning. This, however, makes it the more difficult to understand why Jn. should represent that Jesus was already dead towards five o'clock in the afternoon, for we know that, by no means seldom, crucified men have continued to live on the cross for several days. Further, the lamb had to be chosen on the 10th of Nisan (Exod. xii. 3); in harmony with this, the anointing of Jesus in Bethany, which, according to the Synoptics (Mk. xiv. 8) as well as Jn. (xii. 7), is of the nature of a consecration for his death, is represented in Jn. xii. 1 as taking place on the sixth day before the feast, though Mk. xiv. 1 tells us that it happened on the second day before it (the first and the last day being included; reckoning backwards, therefore, from 15th Nisan as the first day of the feast, this gives us really the 10th Nisan). But, in particular, the day on which the lamb had to be slain was the 14th Nisan (Ex. xii. 6), and this now explains the whole dislocation which Jn. has introduced into the last events of Jesus' life. In the interest of an idea, to Jn. an idea of some importance, Jesus has been made to carry out to the exact letter, in his own person, the whole fate of the paschal lamb, in order to show that all the injunctions concerning it have now been fulfilled and so abolished for ever, and with them all the commands of the religion of the Old Testament.

It might be doubted whether that Evangelist whose work Clement of Alexandria called--and certainly not unjustly--the pneumatic, or the spiritually-centred, gospel, can have attached such importance to this verbal fulfilment of the Old Testament. Yet Jn. has expressly drawn attention to the fact that when Jesus thighs were not broken, an Old Testament prophecy was fulfilled. And in like manner, it is only he who gives Jesus cry on the cross, "I thirst" (xix. 28), and adds that it was made in fulfilment of a passage in the Old Testament (Ps. xxii. 16). It is only he who tells us (xix. 23 f.) that after Jesus crucifixion his cloak and his tunic were differently disposed of, and who adds here also that this was done in fulfilment of a passage in the Bible, the 19th verse of this same 22nd Psalm: "they divided my raiment among them, and upon my vesture did they cast lots." The Synoptics introduce from this Psalm (besides the cry undoubtedly made by Jesus, "My God, my God, why has thou forsaken me?") other matter that might serve to embellish the story of Jesus passion (Mt. xxvii. 39, 43); but they have rightly understood verse 19 to imply only one action (Mk. xv. 24). Jn., in understanding it of two actions, shows, on the one hand, that he has no idea how often, times without number, in the Old Testament one idea is expressed by two clauses slightly differing from each other, and, on the other hand, how anxious he is to demonstrate in the history of Jesus the literal fulfilment of the Old Testament. Much as he felt himself to be exalted above it, so far as it contains injunctions as to life, yet in so far as the prophecies are concerned, he held fast very tenaciously, just as the apostle Paul did, to the thesis that "the scripture cannot be broken" (x. 35). Jesus says to the Jews in this Gospel (v. 39), "Ye search the Scriptures because ye think that in them ye have eternal life" (that is to say, have received assurance of eternal life), "and these are they which "in reality "bear witness of me" Compare further the quotations in xiii. 18 (compared with xvii. 12), xv. 25, xix. 37, xii. 38, and the reference to the serpent lifted up by Moses in the wilderness as being a symbol of the lifting up of Jesus on the cross in iii. 14 f.; also ii. 17, vi. 31, 45, x. 34.

The matter may therefore be summed up as follows. The Synoptics report that the arrest, condemnation, execution, and burial of Jesus took place on a day on which all these things would be associated with difficulties, but would by no means be impossible; and as to how they could have arrived at this, by mistake or of set purpose, if the day were really another one, no one has yet been able to offer a suggestion which is even remotely probable. In the case of Jn., on the other hand, we can tell point by point how he must have come to fix upon another day, supposing the Synoptics were right. As soon as we have perceived this, the question ought to be decided, Are we obliged to believe Jn. on this one point, even though in everything else we have been able to put so little faith in him?

But if any one persists in giving the preference to Jn. here, we must ask him one more question in conclusion; to what are we to trace the agreement between the last acts in the closing day of Jesus' life and those associated with the paschal lamb? Is it chance? Chance in no less than four points? Any one who has not the courage to say this, should realise that only one supposition remains, and one which has been put forward only by the very strictest believers: God so arranged the course of the Passion that everything in it agreed exactly with the injunctions concerning the paschal lamb, purposing in this way to make men realise that Jesus died as the true paschal lamb, and thus did away with the Jewish feast of the Passover and the whole Jewish religion. This view may be found wholly unacceptable, and yet no defender of the statement of the days as given in Jn. can refuse to accept it, unless he is prepared to see here a really very remarkable accident.

26. THE STORY OF JESUS RESURRECTION.

As to the occurrences after Jesus resurrection, especially as to what transpired at the empty grave, the Fourth Evangelist tells us so much that is not found in the other Gospels that it might easily be supposed we have here the words of an eye-witness. The more so because amongst these statements we find also one to the effect that the disciple whom Jesus loved--and whom to all appearance we might sup pose to be the author of the Gospel--hastened with Peter to the tomb. But if that were so, the story of Mk. (xvi. 1-8) and of Mt. (xxviii. 1-8) would be quite inconceivable.

Their chief variation from Jn.--though in this feature Lk. agrees with him--is found, that is to say, in the statement that the women who find the tomb of Jesus empty are commissioned by an angel to bid the disciples go to Galilee, for there they would see their risen Lord. According to Mt. the latter event afterwards happened, and it must have been narrated by Mk. as well; but the original conclusion to his Gospel has been lost, and a much later supplement (xvi. 9-20) substituted for it. In Lk. and Jn., on the other hand, all the appearances of the risen Lord take place in or near Jerusalem. And this too seems really to be the only natural course. All the Gospels agree that Jerusalem was the place in which Jesus rose, and that the disciples were still staying there on Easter morning. Why, then, should the disciples be advised to go to Galilee in order that they might see Jesus?

But for this very reason Mk. and Mt. could never have been led to tell us of this advice to the disciples to go to Galilee, if they had ever heard that Jesus appeared to the disciples in Jerusalem. In no case, therefore, can this account in Lk. and Jn. be the original one; for, if it had been, Mk. and Mt. would unquestionably have heard and accepted it. On the contrary, they must have known of only one account, to wit, that the appearances of the risen Lord had taken place in Galilee.

Even in their case, however, it is remarkable enough that an angel should have to commission the women at the tomb to bid the disciples go to Galilee; and, as a matter of fact, judged by all that we may suppose to have happened, this story is not plausible. Only, the truth is not to be looked for in Lk. and Jn., but in quite a different quarter. In Mk. (xiv. 50) and Mt., that is to say, we read that when Jesus was arrested all the disciples forsook him and fled. Whither? Hardly to Jerusalem; for there what happened to Peter might only too easily happen to them: they might be identified as followers of Jesus. Mk. (xiv. 27 f.) and Mt., however, give us a further clue. When, shortly before his arrest, Jesus prophesied to the disciples that they would all forsake him, he added, "Howbeit, after I am raised up, I will go before you into Galilee." The idea that he would reach Galilee before them agrees with the account of the angel's advice to the women; but it is really too obvious to see in this statement merely a veiled indication that the disciples made their escape to their native place, Galilee, and that Jesus appeared to them there, simply because they took up their abode there from the day of his resurrection or a little later (the distance is two or three days journey). Peter, too, after his denial of Jesus, would certainly have followed the rest.

The mistake in Mk. and Mt., therefore, is not that they assume the appearances of the risen Lord to have taken place in Galilee, but that they suppose the disciples to have been still in Jerusalem on Easter morning. But it was this very mistake that must have suggested to Lk. and Jn. the necessity of making a change. If the disciples were still in Jerusalem after Jesus resurrection, these two Evangelists could not but suppose that here also Jesus must have appeared to them. But what to their mind, of course, was the correction of an error, in reality simply added to the -first mistake a second which was much greater.

If, however, in view of this, Jn. does not by any means give us the truth on the main point, it is clear that in the details also we cannot expect to find it. For instance, in the story of Thomas, which is so beautiful in itself, but of which the Synoptics know nothing, and the scene of which, moreover, is likewise Jerusalem. In the case of the story of Mary Magdalene, attractive and affecting though it is to persons of delicate feeling, we can detect from a particular expression that it is not original, but a reconstruction of a story told in the Synoptics. In Jn. Mary Magdalene came to the sepulchre alone, and yet she says (xx. 2), "we know not where they have laid him." The plural here is only appropriate if there were several women, as in the Synoptics. In xx. 13, the mistake is avoided; Mary Magdalene says here: "I know not where they have laid him."

And, lastly, the race of Peter and the beloved disciple to the sepulchre! This cannot have happened if the disciples were no longer in Jerusalem. But even if they were still there, we must still insist that the Synoptists never had any knowledge of this race; for, had they had any, who could believe that they would have been silent about it? Moreover, we can see here quite clearly step by step how the statements of the Evangelists developed. Although Mk. and Mt. presuppose that the disciples were still present in Jerusalem, they are quite unaware that any of them has visited the sepulchre (and this will be an echo of the truth that they were no longer in Jerusalem). Lk. already knows something about it, but only in the quite indefinite form (xxiv. 24): "and certain of them that were with us went to the tomb, and found it even so as the women had said, but him they saw not." [6] Jn. already knows the names of the disciples and all the details of their visit to the grave.

And how are these details told? The beloved disciple ran faster than Peter, came first to the grave, and saw the linen cloths lying in it, but did not go in. Peter went in and saw, in addition to the linen cloths, the napkin as well. Afterwards the beloved disciple went in too, saw and believed, that is to say, gained the faith that Jesus had risen. Thus, alternately the one gets an advantage over the other; but, first and last, the beloved disciple appears as the greater.

27. INTRODUCTION OF CONDITIONS OF A LATER PERIOD.

In proportion as it becomes less likely that this could have happened at the tomb of Jesus, the question becomes more pressing, Did it not happen in the later careers of the two disciples? We are reluctant to believe it, and yet it can hardly be otherwise: expression is here given to that later struggle for precedence between the two apostles. Peter excelled the beloved disciple by being bolder and observing more closely the details--of, we may now perhaps say without further ado, the life of Jesus; but in faith, that is to say, in the deeper understanding, the beloved disciple had the advantage.

If any one should still have any scruples about seeing here so bold an introduction of the conditions of a later period into the story of Jesus' life, he will dismiss them, we should think, when he takes into consideration another passage of a similar kind. We refer to the words spoken by Jesus, iv.

35-38, on an occasion when there seemed to be a possibility of winning over the men belonging to the city of the woman of Samaria. The idea with which the author starts, that the fields (that is to say, the field of his operations among the Samaritans) are white already unto harvest, seems appropriate to the situation. But not a single word in the concluding sentence (iv. 38) is suitable. It is not true that, before the disciples, others laboured to win the Samaritans, or that the disciples themselves did so (cp. p. 13)-- to say nothing of the idea that they afterwards entered into the labour of their predecessors. On the other hand, all these sentences are seen at once to be true, if we suppose that Jesus is here speaking of the Christian Mission, and in the way in which some one who was looking back upon the progress of this work during a number of decades would be obliged to speak of it. Then, and then only, is it appropriate to say that the one set of missionaries took the place of the other, and that the later only reaped what the earlier had sown (iv. 37 f.). Here then we can note clearly the careless way in which the author makes Jesus express views which could not have been formed until the much later period in which the author himself lived. But at the same time we can see further that such views do not apply to the Samaritans alone, nor even to them in a special sense, but to all the Gentiles. The author regards the Samaritans-- who, as a matter of fact, were not recognised as fellow-countrymen by the Jews (iv. 9; Lk. xvii. 18)-- simply as representatives of the whole Gentile world; it is in this that he finds the fields white already unto harvest.

Again, the strange metaphor by which Jesus represents himself as the door through which a rightful shepherd comes to his sheep (p. 36) can be understood if we seek the explanation in the circumstances of a later period. And we can easily do this if we follow the clue provided in 1 Jn. iv. 1-3. The shepherds and the robbers contrasted with them, stand for two classes of Christian teacher; the former acknowledge the true faith in Christ, the latter disavow it. Strictly speaking, then, not Jesus himself, but faith in him is the door by which a true teacher seeks admission to the members of the Christian communities, as compared with false teachers who seek to force an entrance into the communities without any such passport, and so in an unlawful way, and try to capture the leadership of them. In the lifetime of Jesus of course these two classes of teacher were not in existence; they did not arise until a much later period. In x. 8, it is true, Jesus says that all teachers who came forward before him were thieves and robbers; but this is an entirely new thought, and the interpretation of the adjoining verses (x. 1-7, 9, 10a) cannot be made to depend upon it. In these verses teachers who came forward before Jesus cannot be meant, simply because they could never have been in a position to use him as a door.

28. PRECISE STATEMENTS OF TIME IN JN.

The last thing which is made to tell in favour of the accuracy and fidelity of the Fourth Gospel consists of a number of passages in which the day, and even the hour, in which something happened is stated much more carefully than in the Synoptics. Thus i. 29, 35, 43; vi. 22; xii. 12 commence "on the following day"; ii. 1 "on the third day"; in i. 39 it is four o'clock in the afternoon when the two first disciples, Andrew and one who is unnamed, join Jesus; in iv. 6 it is twelve o'clock midday, when Jesus sits by Jacob's well in Samaria. The inhabitants of the town of Sychar having invited him to stay with them, he remains two days (iv. 40, 43).

If these passages were shown to any one before he knew the rest of the contents of the Fourth Gospel, he would certainly form the opinion that the author must have been a companion of Jesus and deserves to be absolutely trusted even down to the smallest details. But after what has been said in the preceding paragraphs, it is no longer possible to think this. We have actually found that after Jn. has made a statement which is equally precise in form, namely, that Jesus baptised (iii. 22, 26), a few verses later (iv. 2) he himself withdraws it (p. 55 f.). And what is it that happens on each occasion "on the following day"? In i. 29, 35 f. the Baptist is said to have declared Jesus to be the Lamb of God which will take away the sins of the world; in i. 35-42 Andrew and an unnamed disciple are said to have been the first to become disciples of Jesus, and after them Simon, Andrew's brother, and he is said to have received from Jesus at once, without having given any further proof of his fidelity, the name of honour, Peter, that is to say, "rock." All this is diametrically opposed to the account of the Synoptics (p. 79 f.; Mk. i. 16-20), and has no likelihood in itself; in fact, if the Baptist had already called Jesus the Lamb of God, and Andrew (i. 41) had described him as the Saviour, it is quite impossible that Jesus should not have been recognised to be the Saviour until a relatively late date (see p. 33). But what is the use of the precise statement, that a matter happened "on the following day," if it cannot have happened at all?

The only further question that we can ask is, how can Jn. have come to make such precise statements of time? And to this no other answer is possible but that he wished by this device to indicate more clearly the progress made in his story, or intended the words to introduce another important suggestion. When in chap. i. he has arrived at a new stage in the increase in the number of Jesus' disciples, he says that a new day is beginning. We cannot really be surprised at this in a man who is so little concerned about literal accuracy. It helps to make his story decidedly more vivid and impressive; and it is actually his purpose to paint pictures which will make an impression (see pp. 55 f. and 96 f.).

The question whether the statements about Jesus journeys to the feasts (p. 9 f.) have arisen in the same way, or were actually "delivered" to Jn., we must leave undecided.

The hours of the day in i. 39, iv. 6, which we mentioned above, may perhaps have a hidden meaning. If we cannot define it, it does not in the least follow that we have before us the account of an eye-witness. We have quite clearly a hidden meaning of the kind in vi. 4, when we are told that at the time of the feeding of the five thousand "the feast of the Passover was near." The discourses which follow are an explanation of the Supper (see p. 98). No one, however, could have known this, since the Supper does not take place in Jn., and in the Synoptics not until a year later. It must, therefore, have been hinted at in a hidden, though intelligible, way. With this, however, agrees the statement, that the Passover was near; for it was at a Passover festival that Jesus celebrated the Supper with his disciples. If this be correct, there would no longer be any occasion to consider seriously the idea that Jesus' ministry lasted for two years; for this is based entirely upon the statement about this feast of the Passover (p. 9 f.). But the idea also that it began shortly before a (preceding) feast of the Passover is simply founded on the fact that the expulsion of the dealers from the fore-court of the Temple, which Jn . transfers from the end to the beginning of the public work of Jesus, according to the account of the Synoptics happened at a Passover feast. The short space of two days, for which, according to iv. 40, 43, Jesus accepted the invitation to stay in the Samaritan town agrees with the time beyond which in the second century a travelling preacher was not allowed to stay as a guest and receive board.

CONCLUSION.

But enough. A book in which Jesus gives the explanation of the Supper a year before its celebration; in which 500, if not 1000, soldiers, when he whom they are sent to take prisoner says "I am he," recoil and fall to the ground (xviii. 3-6); in which one hundred pounds of spices are used to embalm his body (xix. 39), ought, at the outset, to be safe from the misunderstanding that it recounts real events. These three points are enough to show that it is dominated by complete indifference as to the faithfulness of a record; that importance is attached only to giving as impressive a representation as possible of certain ideas; and that the whole is sustained by a reverence of Jesus which has lost every standard for measuring what can really happen.

Footnotes:

5. Further information on this subject will be found in Seydel, Das Evangelium von Jesu in semen Verhältnissen zu Buddha-Sage und Buddha-Lehre, 1882, pp. 239-251.

6. Lk. xxiv. 12, according to which Peter ran to the tomb, saw the linen cloths lying, and departed to his home, wondering, certainly did not originally find a place in the Third Gospel but was only added to it subsequently as an abstract from the Fourth. Only, in Lk. the beloved disciple was ignored, because he was not known at all to the readers of the Third Gospel.

CHAPTER IV - FUNDAMENTAL IDEAS OF THE FOURTH GOSPEL AND THEIR ORIGINS

FROM all that we have said so far, it may have become more and more obvious, that what is decisive, in the thought and in the presentation of the Fourth Evangelist, is the conception of Jesus which exists in his own mind. This idea we must now follow up more closely if we are to advance from a mere comparison of Jn.'s picture of Jesus' life with that of the Synoptics, and from the conclusion that it deserves less belief, to the most underlying reasons why he has left us so incorrect a description of Jesus' life.

For this purpose, in the first place we shall deal with a section of his book about which we have not yet spoken because the Synoptics do not contain one like it, we mean the prologue, i. 1-18. Something to which hitherto our attention has only been directed occasionally--the fact that Jesus before his earthly life lived a life with God in heaven--is here, at the very outset and with the greatest emphasis, placed at the head of everything, and is even surpassed by the explanation, "he was the word" (in Greek "the logos").

1. REVELATION THROUGH "THE WORD" (THE LOGOS).

This remarkable expression has had a history of its own, and would in itself have quite justified the publishers of the Religionsgeschichtliche Volksbücher in allowing the Fourth Gospel a separate treatment. In all religions, it has been found again and again that the deity, if men are to learn to know its will and to aim at following it, must reveal itself. This it does, according to the belief of different peoples, in very different ways. But when it does so, for example, by natural events, by serious misfortunes, men do not know at first what they on their part ought to do in order to remove its anger. Special means are needed to find this out. Wise men must explain the will of God, whether they read it in the stars or in the flight of birds or in the entrails of sacrificial animals, or in whatever it may be. The prospect of doing this is far more auspicious, if there are prophets with whom God--as they themselves are convinced--really speaks in their inner man, in such a way that they can directly reproduce God's very words. It is not without reason, for example, that Muhammed in the Koran again and again emphasises the fact that he has proclaimed to his people "in clear Arabic" the will of God. But in the Old Testament, in which we have such abundant information about the prophets, there are "false" prophets besides the "true"; yet these quite certainly considered themselves to be the true, and the distinction between the two classes was of such real difficulty, that rules are given about it in the Bible itself which are quite impracticable and even contradictory (Deut. xviii. 20-22; xiii. 2-6). Clearly then the most helpful thing that could happen would be for a divine being, who could not make mistakes, to appear himself upon earth in order to speak immediately with men. Such a being would really deserve to be called the incarnate "word of God."

2. THE LOGOS AS REASON.

The Greek expression for "word" (logos), however, means at the same time "reason." This brings us to a second origin of this name for Jesus, and one which lies not so much in religion as in the contemplation of the Greek philosophers about the world as a whole. If we recognise in this world one order, it is natural to say that this world, as well as each individual man, possesses a "reason." The logos is then the reasonable order which rules in the world, and so we are able to express ourselves, even if we cannot believe that the world is ruled by a deity who possesses a consciousness of himself.

In this sense Heraclitus (about 500-450 B.C.) introduced the term "logos" into Greek philosophy. Plato (427-347), without using this term, assumed a world of ideas in which the highest, the idea of the Good, represents the deity. These ideas he regards as the original patterns of which all particular things in the material world are only copies. The Stoics (from 300 B.C.) adopted the word logos and the idea of Heraclitus, that the logos is the reasonable order that rules in the world. On this view, therefore, particular things are adapted to the logos, just as, on Plato's view, they are to the ideas. In correspondence with the plurality of ideas in Plato, the Stoics divided the one logos into a plurality, which is called in Greek logoi. To the statement that these logoi are the originals or patterns of the things in the world, they added a second statement, that they are the powers by which the things of the world are established. So they compare the logoi with seeds of corn which have been scattered everywhere in the world and which have produced out of themselves the particular things. Thus it happens, on their view, that the deity which they see in the one logos, the world-reason, through its particular logoi creates all that is, in conformity with that original which it actually represents itself.

We find the doctrine of the logos fully developed in the Jewish thinker Philo, who was twenty to thirty years older than Jesus. In his native city, Alexandria, in Egypt, he had the best opportunity of imbibing Greek philosophy, and of combining it with the ideas which he himself cherished as a Jew. Consequently, the logos is the pattern and producer of things, as we found it on Greek soil; but it cannot be the deity himself (that would conflict with Philo's Jewish faith); it is simply a second divine being, who is subordinate to the God of the Old Testament.

In the Old Testament itself we also find the beginnings of a disposition to distinguish between God himself and a second divine being of this kind. In particular, the Wisdom of God is often represented as assisting God at the creation of the world; it then works in his sight for his delight (Job xxviii. 12-28; Proverbs viii. 22-31; Ecclus. i. 1-10; xxiv. 1-12; Wisdom of Solomon vii. 22-30). This is, of course, only a figurative way of saying that God at the creation of the world made use of his wisdom; but the form of the world, which he conceived in this wisdom of his, before he made the real to arise in conformity with the ideal, may, with a little imagination, be regarded as the original of the world as it existed in the abstract, or as a kind of model of it. And we get some thing very like the expression "logos," when it is said that God created the world by his word (Psalm xxxiii. 6), because in Gen. i. 3 it is said, "God spake . . . and it was so." In the Hebrew Old Testament as translated into the Aramaic language current at the time of the Fourth Evangelist, and as recited in the Synagogue every Sabbath, in place of the name God, which the people had to avoid pronouncing, the expression "the word of God" was often put, even where, strictly speaking, it was not suitable.

All this, and presumably in addition, legends about the gods, who, according to the religions of Egypt, Babylonia, or Greece, as the agents of a still higher Deity shaped the world and filled it with divine effects, Philo sums up, by representing that the Logos in itself was, on the one hand, only a faculty of God, by which he conceived the organisation of the world, and, on the other hand, a being who has come forth from God and brought God's influence into the world. In the second sense, we can call it a person, but in the former not; and the important point is that in Philo the Logos must always be a person and at the same time not a person. Were it only the one or only the other, some necessary aspect which it has would be neglected. Philo gives the Logos designations which only seem applicable to a person; for example, the first-born son of God, the high-priest, the mediator, the sinless one. We must not lose sight of the fact, however, that it always remains the power of mind in God.

3. JESUS AS LOGOS IN THE NEW TESTAMENT EPISTLES.

The idea has played a further part in the history of religion in the New Testament itself. The Fourth Evangelist, that is to say, is by no means the first New Testament writer to represent Jesus as the Logos; others did the same before him. Even Paul presupposes that, before Jesus appeared on earth, he lived a life with God in heaven (Gal iv. 4; Rom. x. 6). In doing so, he thinks of him, in spite of all his heavenly perfection, as a man in whose image earthly beings, especially men, were first created (1 Cor. xv. 45-49; xi. 8). In fact, according to one passage (1 Cor. viii. 6), he himself helped to carry out the creation of the world. In any case, he arose in quite a different way from human beings, and for this reason he is called God's own son (Rom. viii. 32). We can see how much there is here in agreement with Philo, whose writings or ideas Paul may have known very well. However, it is noteworthy that Paul was not so much concerned, as Philo was, to explain the origin of the whole world; had he been, he would have described Jesus as the prototype of the whole world and not merely of human beings.

The Epistle to the Hebrews, whose author unquestionably knew Philo's writings, takes us a step further. To him Christ, before he descended upon earth, is no longer a man in heaven, but is a reflexion of the majesty and imprint of the nature of God, just as in a seal the imprint entirely resembles the stamp; he has not only created the world, but he also continually sustains it; that is to say, keeps it in existence (i. 2 f. 10). The manner in which he proceeded from God is expressly described as a "being begotten" (i. 5), and he is accordingly called simply "Son of God," without further addition, and so with the implication that there is only one such (i. 1 f. 5; not so, however, in i. 6 "the first-born"). It is all the more note worthy that Jesus "in the days of his flesh offered up prayers and supplications with strong crying and tears unto him that was able to save him from death, and . . . though he was a Son, yet learned obedience by the things which he suffered" (v. 7 f.), and that he "in all points like as we," men, "was tempted, yet without sin" (iv. 15), This true recollection of real events in the life of Jesus can only be reconciled with the description of his God-like elevation before his earthly existence by supposing, as Paul does in 2 Cor. viii. 9 and Phil. ii. 6 f., that when he descended upon earth he emptied himself of his heavenly powers, and assumed the form of a man, even of a servant.

The Epistle to the Colossians (the most important sections of which cannot have been written by Paul himself) adds to the two statements, that through Christ the world was made and is maintained in existence, a third to the effect that it was created for him, so that he is thus its goal (i. 15-17). Moreover, it calls him the image of the invisible God, and in doing so, explains even more clearly than the Epistle to the Hebrews why God needed such an image. But, above all, in the Epistle to the Colossians we find the idea of the humiliation of Jesus on earth inter changed with its opposite. It is said in ii. 9, "in him dwells the fulness of the Godhead bodily"; and this is true, not merely from the time of Jesus resurrection, but even during his heavenly life before his earthly existence, and then even during his earthly life itself. We read for instance in i. 19 f., God "was pleased that in him should all the fulness dwell, and wished" (afterwards) "through him to reconcile all things unto himself, having made peace through the blood of his cross, &c." If the author had thought as Paul did, he would not, directly before the mention of Jesus' sacrificial death, have emphasised the fact that God endowed Jesus with all the fulness of the God head. The whole of the Gospel of Jn. is an amplification of this briefly suggested thought, that in Jesus all the fulness of the Godhead dwelt on earth, as in heaven.

4. MINGLING OF RELIGIONS AT THE TIME OF JN.

Before, however, we can show this, it remains necessary to review another part of the history of religion; that is to say, the mingling of the religions of the Babylonians, Persians, Egyptians, Syrians, people of Asia Minor and Greeks, in the last centuries before Christ. Amongst nearly all these peoples there were legends of gods, goddesses or sons of gods, who came down from heaven to earth to contend with hostile beings. One such foe is the great serpent of the Babylonian religion. It represents darkness, and the floods which in that country made the winter such a joyless season. It is conquered by the sun of spring, which is of course thought of as a god. In other religions the struggle associated with the change in the year's seasons was differently represented, but in such a way that the identity of the thing could not be mistaken.

Another purpose for which the gods had to descend from heaven is found in the belief that the soul of man is from heaven and yearns after its home, but cannot find the way, unless a being descends from above and releases it from the prison in which it is held captive. This idea also had received, in different religions, different, but not altogether dissimilar, expression.

But even that the world might be created or organised, subordinate divine beings had to help as soon as a religion was dominated by the belief that the highest God, if He was to continue to be perfectly pure and divine, could have nothing to do with the world.

But, further, it must be possible to say, as regards these divine beings, how they arose; and their origin, as can be easily understood, was represented in such a way that one always proceeded from the other or was born from two others, thought of as male and female. Here we have reason enough for the existence of a number of divine figures in every religion, whose derivation from one another, whose rank, friendship and enmity amongst one another, whose activity in favour or to the detriment of men, it was a somewhat intricate problem to solve.

When, especially from the end of the fourth century, Alexander the Great's expeditions brought all the well-known peoples, and many more which were less important, into frequent contact, there was an interchange of ideas, even as regards their gods. The agreement between so many divine forms in the different religions was recognised, and the manner in which such and such a god was worshipped in one country was transferred to the related god in another, so long as people believed that, by doing so, they could better assure themselves of his help. In brief, a complete mingling started, which made this whole world of deities not only an intricate, but even a confused, puzzle.

5. GNOSTICISM.

Gnosticism drew upon this mingling of religions. This was a very important movement, but is so difficult to present in detail that we must be content to give only the most noteworthy outlines. Gnosis means "knowledge"; and this is in fact the first and most important point, that one must have a great fund of knowledge to be able to know all these doctrines about the different divine beings, and at the same time a great deal of penetration rightly to apprehend the deep thoughts which were hidden under such wonderful clothing. These Gnostics, or Knowers, were at the same time men who thought deeply about the origin of the world; and their ideas were again taken up by several of the most prominent philosophers of the nineteenth century.

One idea which continually recurs in their systems is that a deep division runs through the world. God is by nature good, pure, unspotted; the matter of which the world consists is also by nature evil, impure, tainted. God cannot therefore come into contact with this matter; and it would have remained for ever unorganised and devoid of any divine influence, if subordinate divine beings had not imparted this to it and converted it into an organised world. They do it, however, in a very imperfect way; for their own knowledge is quite limited. This is why the world is so faulty.

The soul and the body of men are by nature just as much strangers to one another as are God and the world. The soul comes from heaven, whether it be supposed that the creator of the world, that is to say, one of those divine, but subordinate, beings, created it, or that it represents a spark which emanated from the highest God Himself and descended into the gloomy kingdom of the world. The body, however, is a part of that matter of which the world consists, and therefore shares all its evil characteristics. Through the senses, and the spell which they exercise, it drags down the soul into the domain of the vile and common, and estranges it from its divine destiny. It is its prison, and the soul cannot escape from it, partly for the very good reason that it is no longer conscious of its divine origin. If, therefore, it is to be redeemed, some one must come who will first make it realise that it has come from God. But this can only be a being who has himself come from God, and possesses the knowledge of the divine in full measure--in other words, a god.

All Gnostics who confessed themselves Christians have found this being in Christ as he appeared upon earth. But the division which exists between the soul and the body of every man, of course affects him also, and even in a much stronger degree. A being so high and divine cannot really have a body which consists of earthly matter. Consequently, the Gnostics could only explain in one of two ways. Either the Christ who came down from heaven was only in an external way united to an ordinary man Jesus, who was born of Joseph and Mary, but was righteous in a peculiar degree: that is to say, he came down upon him at the baptism in the Jordan, but left him again before he suffered death, so that the person who underwent suffering was only the man Jesus. Or the heavenly Christ, during the whole of his sojourn upon earth, possessed himself of a phantom body, so that all his human acts, such as eating, sleeping, suffering, &c., were nothing more than appearance.

From what we have said, it will be clear that the chief task of this redeemer was to make the soul of man realise that it is of divine origin. But many souls are not able to apprehend this truth; and so the same disastrous division again makes itself felt, and separates men into two classes. In the nature of the case, it is very conceivable that the great sum of knowledge and the great depth of thought appertaining to Gnosis, could not be within the reach of many simple people. But the Gnostics assumed that the question who can attain to it has been decided long before one comes to know it; from eternity there are some, namely the Gnostics themselves, endowed with the capacity to appropriate it as soon as it is imparted to them, whereas to others this faculty is denied from eternity, and therefore they could never be happy.

From the time when the soul of the Gnostic comes to know its divine origin it is, strictly speaking, released from its fetters. A new life begins for it, and from this point it is already sure of returning to heaven as soon as death emancipates it from the body. For this reason, in 2 Tim. ii. 18, and of course in a tone of reproach, the doc trine of the Gnostics is represented thus: "the resurrection is come already." And it is a resurrection only of the soul. The body can in no way share in the eternal happiness; it abides for ever in death. The Gnostics are equally firm in rejecting the idea that the Christ, who has risen and been exalted to heaven, will return to earth again, when the dead will be awakened and their works judged. Every soul at the moment of death of itself reaches its final state of happiness.

6. THE PROLOGUE OF THE FOURTH GOSPEL.

We may now turn to the opening words of the Gospel of Jn. They read: "In the beginning was the Logos, and the Logos was with God, and the Logos was God. The same was in the beginning with God. All things were made by him; and without him was not anything made that hath been made." None of these statements is now new to us. Only, we must guard against misunderstanding the third, as if it meant: God himself was the same being as the Logos--which in fact would not agree with what has already been mentioned. It would be equally wrong to make the statement mean the contrary: the Logos was a god. The sense is rather: the Logos was of divine nature (just as in iv. 24 the words "God is spirit" mean: God is of a spiritual nature, has a spiritual nature). This is really what we should expect: the Logos is not God Himself, but of like nature. Similarly, we may expect that he was from the beginning, and so existed before the creation of the world, and with God, and that by him the whole world was made. What Paul, the Epistle to the Hebrews, and the Epistle to the Colossians have said with increasing precision, only without using the word Logos, is here expressed by the Fourth Evangelist quite in the language of Philo.

It should therefore never have been doubted that Jn. borrowed the word Logos and the ideas associated with it from Philo. And if we were inclined to take offence that such an important idea should have come to the Biblical author from an extra-Biblical writer--though in truth there is nothing objectionable in it--yet we can console ourselves with the thought that Jn. has shown great independence. He continues in verse 14, "and the Logos became flesh, and dwelt among us." The idea that the Logos could become flesh would have been to Philo something impossible. We see then that Jn. gives the idea an entirely new turn. Only, it would be a misunderstanding to interpret it: the Logos was transformed into flesh. The sentence is certainly opposed to the idea of the Gnostics, according to which the Christ who had come down from heaven was not a real man. But Jn., nevertheless, agrees with them inasmuch as he thinks the transformation of a divine being into a fleshly being cannot be imagined. A more guarded statement therefore would be: he became man, or as we read in 1 Jn. iv. 2 and 2 Jn. 7, he came in the flesh that is to say, not "he came into flesh," but "he came, clothed with flesh; he came forward with a body consisting of flesh." It is possible that, as against the Gnostics, the expression "he became flesh" was a more sharp than useful definition from the point of view of clearness.

In other places also it is clear that Jn. does not on all points reject the ideas of the Gnostics. Certainly he will not hear of their many divine beings, but knows of the one true God and of Jesus Christ whom he has sent (xvii. 3). But this Christ is to him, as to the Gnostics, a necessary mediator between God and the world, and in his view, exactly as in theirs, he must for a definite time appear upon earth. These last ideas are, it is true, shared also by Paul, the Epistle to the Hebrews, and the Epistle to the Colossians; the first especially by the Epistle to the Colossians, in which God, just as in Jn. i. 18, vi. 46, is an invisible God and Christ his image (Col. i. 15). But what Jn. has in common with the Gnostics alone is the idea that it was Christ's most important work to communicate a certain kind of knowledge to men.

At the end of i. 14: "and we beheld his glory, glory as of the only begotten from the Father, full of grace and truth," we have, further, the most peculiar term which Jn. applies to Jesus to describe precisely the sense in which he is the Son of God. The Greek word monogenes means the only son w r ho was begotten by his father, and that, in ordinary human relations, means of course the single son produced by a father. This being so, a satisfactory translation would be: "the only son." Since, however, in Jn.'s Gospel, by the side of Jesus as the Son of God, there appear very many children of God among men, the second part of the expression also acquires a special sense: Jesus is the only son of God who was begotten by Him; all others have been produced by Him in another way.

Thus we must understand the idea of the author--even though just before he has spoken of men who are able to be come children of God, and has used a related Greek expression to the effect that they were begotten from God. Those are meant of whom the Gnostics say they are able to apprehend the idea of their heavenly origin because they come from God. But that Jn. thought of Christ as having arisen in another way, having been begotten in a more peculiar sense, is seen already in the persistence with which he applies the name "son" solely to him, and always calls all others the children of God (see p. 64).

But at the same time he has perhaps chosen the name monogenés, because several Gnostics, in their long list of divine beings, used it of a being different from the Logos, that is to say, of an older being and one standing in a closer relationship to God. Of him Jn. will not hear.

7. JESUS AS LOGOS THROUGHOUT THE FOURTH GOSPEL.

But the most important feature in this expression, "we saw his majesty," &c. (i. 14) is this, that the whole Gospel is nothing but an amplification of it, This explains the continual insistence on the omnipotence and omniscience of Jesus, the omission of the baptism, the temptation, the anguish in Gethsemane; it explains the prayer at the grave of Lazarus, which was only for the sake of the people, the saying on the cross "I thirst," which was only in fulfilment of a passage in the Bible, Jesus inviolability when attempts were made to capture or to stone him, the falling down of the Roman battalion when he said "I am he" whom ye seek, his continual reference to his own person and to his life with God before his descent upon earth, his ambiguous style of speaking without considering whether his hearers could follow him, his continual demand that they must believe in him, his continual assurance that only faith in him could give eternal life; his unvarying uniformity from beginning to end, his opposition to "the Jews" without distinction, his superiority to "the law of the Jews" and "the feasts of the Jews," and the colourlessness of the figure of the Baptist, who is only permitted to point to Jesus. This explains, in particular, certain utterances of Jesus which we have not yet mentioned: "And now (that is to say, now that I am taking farewell of the earth), Father, glorify thou me with thine own self, with the glory which I had with thee before the world was" (xvii. 5), "before Abraham was, I am" (viii. 58). The "I am" seems really to be senseless. But, as a matter of fact, there is a purpose in it, and it alone gives the sentence its real force. Strictly speaking, two sentences have been compressed into one: "before Abraham was, I was" and "I am eternal and, being such, have no change." Next and last, iii. 13, "No man hath ascended into heaven" in order to bring information, "but he only" can bring it "who descended out of heaven, the Son of man, which is in heaven," that is to say "who is simultaneously in heaven continually," not "who was in heaven." The four last words are omitted in important manuscripts, but only, we may be sure, because the copyists thought they went too far. They very appropriately reflect Jn.'s idea about Jesus, and were therefore certainly written by him. Finally, the positive summing-up of Jn.'s view is expressed by Thomas in the last words addressed to Jesus in the Fourth Gospel (xx. 28), "My Lord and my God." In the rest of the New Testament Jesus is called "God" only in Heb. i. 8 f. (Tit. ii. 13?); in 1 Tim. iii. 16; Rom. ix. 5, he is only so called through a wrong reading or faulty punctuation.

8. SUPPRESSION OF HUMAN TRAITS IN JESUS.

From tins can now be gathered how greatly Jn.'s style of thinking is misunderstood when an attempt is made to find traits of a real humanity in the Jesus of the Fourth Gospel. Those who do this, for instance, in the case of the raising of Lazarus, or those even who are only disturbed by the thought that no such traits can really be found, have quite misunderstood the peculiar character of this book. Humanly speaking, Jesus must have been so cruel as to keep away from Bethany for two more days, because otherwise the miracle which he proposed to do would not have been so great as if it did not happen until the fourth day after Lazarus' death. We ought not. however, to apply this human point of view; if we are to do the Evangelist justice, we ought, just as he does, to identify our selves to such an extent with this Son of God who has come from heaven, as to approve entirely of his demonstrating his exaltation, his dignity, and his omnipotence in the strongest possible way. So long as it is what is truly human in Jesus that attracts us, we are totally unfit to enter into the ideas of the Evangelist, for he is attracted only by what is divine.

This is, in fact, so much the case that the human in Jesus is more sternly set aside than the Evangelist himself desires. He would like certainly to oppose the Gnostics, amongst whom the heavenly Christ was united with the man Jesus only superficially and for a limited period, or only had a phantom body to deceive the eyes of men. To meet this latter idea, he insists that there flowed from the wound, which was made by the spear-thrust in the crucified Lord, blood and water (xix. 34); and perhaps he has the same thing in mind when he says that Jesus sat down tired by Jacob's well (iv. 6), and so forth. In this Gospel again Jesus speaks of having always observed the commands of God (xv. 10) and of being studious to do not his own will, but the will of God (v. 30). But how does all this help us? This kind of obedience can hardly be said to have the same value as the obedience of a man to God, for Jesus simply could not act otherwise; he himself speaks of doing the will of God as being his food (iv. 34). He can even say "I and the Father are one" (x. 30); and the reason for this is not that he entirely subordinates his own will to the will of his heavenly Father (he does indeed do this, but only because it was natural for him to do so), but that he, and he alone, was begotten of God, that he, and he alone, was of like nature with God.

This is as clear as daylight, when he walks over the sea, or when, on an attempt being made to stone him, he makes himself invisible in a miraculous way; when his soul is affected by no feelings of passion; when he keeps away for two days from the place where his friend has died, in order to set his miraculous power in a brighter light; when Philip is made to see in his person, as he stands before him, God the Father. Here he is actually, in hardly a different way than he is amongst the Gnostics, a God walking upon the earth, whom one can only worship in astonishment. A man whose possibilities are exposed to limitations, as those of others are, who thinks and feels like others, to whom one can cling, because he has first trodden the same path and experienced the same difficulties, whom one can gladly follow--no, he is nothing of this. The Fourth Gospel knows nothing and can know nothing of the great consolation which the Epistle to the Hebrews (ii. 18) gives to all such earthly pilgrims: "because that he himself hath suffered, being tempted, he is able to succour them that are tempted."

Nevertheless, we shall refuse to reproach its author for this, in proportion as it becomes clear to us that the task which he set before himself was from the first impossible of achievement. Nor has any later teacher in the Church been able so to reconcile the divine and human nature in Jesus, that a real and consistent personality has been produced. The important point, therefore, is simply to recognise on which of the two sides in Jn. the scale turns. Those who persist in attempting to reconcile the two natures, are not agreed, even down to the present day, as to whether they ought to say, as Paul says (see above, p. 146), that Jesus, when he came down from heaven to earth, laid aside his divine characteristics, or that he kept them, hiding them during his earthly life. As regards the Fourth Gospel, we must say that it quite certainly does not take the first of these positions. And even as regards the second view, it only presents the thought that on earth Jesus was endowed with all his divine characteristics; their concealment is very slight and transparent, and does not really accord with the purpose of Jesus' public ministry, which in Jn. consists simply in revealing himself in all his greatness.

9. KINGDOM OF GOD AND KINGDOM OF THE DEVIL ACCORDING TO JN.

Although the figure of Jesus claims almost the whole attention of the Fourth Gospel, we must, in order to realise its fundamental ideas and discover their origin, look into Jn.'s answer to the question, What is God's relation to the world, and the world's relation to God? We have been obliged to touch upon this already; for the whole descent of Christ from heaven to earth would not have been necessary, if God by His own work had made the world according to His will. There is, therefore, in Jn., strictly speaking, exactly the same deep division between God and the world as exists in the system of the Gnostics. And to this he gives expression often enough.

Two kingdoms, we should almost say two worlds, are contrasted, the one which is above, and the one which is below; from the one is Jesus, from the other are the Jews (viii. 23). This lower kingdom is also called the earth; it is, therefore, quite literally supposed that Jesus came down from that heaven which forms an arch over the earth (iii. 31). Elsewhere, the lower kingdom is called also "this world," or simply "the world"; heaven is consequently never included in it. The upper kingdom is that of light, truth, life; to the lower belong darkness, deception, and death (i. 5; iii. 19-21; viii. 44; vi. 47-54). The ruler of the upper kingdom is, of course, God; the ruler of the lower is the devil (viii. 44). Paul also has already called the devil the god of this world (2 Cor. iv. 4), but he has not set up any thing like so harsh an opposition between it and the kingdom of heaven. In Jn. this opposition is based on the thought that God cannot come into contact with the world, because the matter of which it consists is evil by nature and God would be denied by any contact with it. This idea is not only represented in the Gnostic system, but is found even in Plato, and has thence become the common property of many Greek philosophers, and, in particular, of the Jews also who, like Philo, made the philosophic thinking of the Greeks their own.

10. CHILDREN OF GOD AND OF THE DEVIL.

The consequence, strictly speaking, was that all men were incapable of receiving any divine gift. But the other idea also, which we have found among the Gnostics, that the souls of men come from the upper kingdom, was very widespread. But not all souls. And so the Gospel of Jn. reveals that deep division, which separates God and the world, even between those men who are begotten from God (i. 13), and those who are the children of the devil (viii. 44). It is only another mode of expressing this, when it is said in iii. 6, "that which is born of the flesh is flesh, and that which is born of the spirit is spirit." And this sentence would lose all force, if we were to continue: but that also which is born of the flesh can become spirit and vice versâ. If it is to have any value, we must complete it thus: that which is born of the flesh is and remains flesh, and that which is born of the spirit is and remains spirit. Further it accords entirely with this when in viii. 47 it is said: "ye hear not" the words of God, "because ye are not of God," or in viii. 43, "ye cannot hear my word?" or in vi. 65, "No man can come unto me, except it be given unto him of the Father." And when he is leaving the earth, Jesus utters those words in xvii. 9 which may well startle us: "I pray not for the world, but for those whom thou hast given me." In fact, if this were the Evangelist's last word, he could not be distinguished from a Gnostic; only destined men could come to know the truth, and redemption would consist merely in enabling these alone to recognise their heavenly origin and so to achieve their emancipation from the prison formed by their body.

11. SOFTENING OF THE OPPOSITION,.

The Evangelist, however, does not actually go so far. He already declares against the Gnostics when in i. 3 he says that by the Logos the world was made, and so not, as they taught, by subordinate divine beings, who had no correct understanding of the way to do it, but by the highest and only representative of God. True, if we were inclined to conclude from this, that this Being must have made it quite according to God's will, it would certainly be hard to under stand why, notwithstanding, it is a kingdom of darkness, deception, and death. The division between God and the world, which the author has accepted from the philosophical thinkers of his time, is therefore not really set aside; but the author has made a move in this direction.

In the next place, we are told in v. 22, in the spirit of the same harsh division between God and the world, that God judges no one, but has committed the whole work of judging to the Son. As regards other works, however, he does not deny that God exercises them in the world; for example, God attracts to Jesus the men who from the beginning were destined to come to him (vi. 44). But we have, in quite a special way, the expression "world," in which the change of Jn.'s mode of thought is revealed. When Jesus declines to pray for the world (xvii. 9), the world includes only those men who are children of the devil. Similarly, in xv. 19, "be cause ye are not of the world, . . . therefore the world hates you." Between these two parts of the sentence, however, we have the clause, "because I have chosen you from the world," and here the word "world "has a wider sense; it includes all men, even those who, since they could be chosen, were from the first children of God, and therefore, according to the more limited use of the word, are not "of the world." Similarly in xvii. 6, "I manifested thy name unto the men whom thou gavest me out of the world." But expressions like that in iii. 16 f. go even beyond these: "For God so loved the world that he gave his only begotten son, that whosoever believeth on him should not perish, but have eternal life. For God sent not the Son into the world to judge the world; but that the world should be saved through him": that is to say the whole world, and not merely individuals singled out of the world (similarly xii. 47; i. 29; vi. 33).

12. DIFFERENCE BETWEEN JN. AND THE GNOSTICS.

The importance of these differences between Jn. and the Gnostics cannot be overstated. By its very nature, Gnosticism was unable to make itself master of the world, because it was, and aimed at being, a religion restricted to a limited number of privileged persons. The simple man, the simple woman, could never hope to be numbered amongst these. All the valuable and exalted elements contained in the Gospel of Jn. could only be saved for the Church, and so for all future times, by the author's declaring them to be destined for all men. "God willeth that all men should be saved, and come to the knowledge of the truth": this saying (1 Tim. ii. 4) possesses telling force; and the author of the Fourth Gospel has not failed to notice it.

It was not less important, however, that he should have differed from the Gnostics in his teaching about the creation of the world. The belief in one God could not be held to consistently if one of the most important kinds of work which the pious gladly ascribe to Him, the creation of the world, was carried out in a very faulty way by subordinate and unintelligent beings. Many Gnostics went so far as to see in this unintelligent creator of the world the God of the Old Testament of whom it is said, that he produced the world. He was then regarded by them as a being quite different from the real God.

In consequence, however, the Old Testament, which was likewise regarded as his work, seemed at the same time to be a useless and abortive book, though at that time it was the only holy book which Christians who adhered to the Church .had (the New Testament writings were not regarded as holy until towards the end of the second century, and in large part had not yet been written at the time when Gnosticism made its way into the Christian communities, that is to say, about the year 100). By such ideas, simple Christians, who on all questions thought they might rely on the Old Testament, were thoroughly confused. It is perhaps for this reason that the author of the Gospel of Jn. emphasises the statement that Holy Scripture could not be annulled (see p. 129). The Gnostics supposed that it was quite a new revelation which Christ brought from heaven; if, however, as Jn. represents, this Christ was the same being who had made the world, simple believers might rest assured that everything which they received as a revelation through the Old Testament and the teaching of Christianity was in agreement.

As regards this Christ, however, if one followed the Gnostics, one could not take seriously what Christian tradition had to communicate concerning his life upon earth. Take, for example, the death on the cross. It was this, according to the common belief of the Church, that brought salvation to mankind; but according to the Gnostics another person, an ordinary man, must be supposed to have suffered, or the body of Christ was merely a phantom figure. In this way, the whole foundation of the faith of the Church crumbled to pieces. It was of the highest importance to receive the assurance that it really was the redeemer himself who was concerned in all the records of the Gospel story.

And this was all the more important, because the existence of the Church at that time was very seriously endangered. On the one side, the Gnostics attracted a large following. On the other, the old habit of worshipping the pagan deities and a continued intercourse with relatives and friends who had remained pagan, enticed people back to the old beliefs. Above all, however, the persecutions of Christians, which from the beginning of the second century followed upon one another all too quickly, made it really difficult for the young community to persist in its faith. And though we, at the present time, reject so much that was at that time accounted a necessary part of Christianity, and has perhaps been clung to with a tenacity which may be vexatious to us, yet, in judging past periods, we ought never to forget one thing, that something which we can dispense with to-day may at an earlier date have been in dispensable because people had not anything better to cling to, and that perhaps we might not have had Christianity as a whole to-day if in time of danger it had not been kept intact by means which we should no longer think of using. Had the martyrs, for example those at Lyons in the year 177, not cherished so firmly the conviction that God would bring together from the ocean every particle of the ashes of their burnt bodies, which the Romans scattered in the Rhone in mockery of their faith, and so at the resurrection would completely reunite their bodies with the old shapes, who can say whether they would have endured their terrible tortures with that firmness which made their persecutors on the very next day adopt the same faith and themselves go to death on its behalf?

13. JN.'S LEANING TO THE TEACHING OF THE CHURCH.

When the author of the Fourth Gospel takes up another position, different from that of the Gnostics and more akin to the faith of the Church, arid yet in many points agrees with them we would like much to know whether this mingling is due entirely to a want of clearness or whether it admits of a more satisfactory explanation. At that time, when so many competing ideas were brought to the notice of the individual, it is not inconceivable that many persons might appropriate something of one and some thing of another, without being able really to blend the two. Many other persons, however, will have attached themselves entirely to the one at first, and afterwards have had a leaning to the other, without having given up everything that at an earlier time they had accepted as true. We may suppose the author of our Gospel to have been in this position. Not that he was in process of passing from the teaching of the Church to Gnosticism, but, on the contrary, of passing from Gnosticism to the teaching of the Church. This, of course, is merely a conjecture. It, however, strikes us as probable, because we may presume that the Gnostic ideas would be more prominent and not so strongly combated if the author had been by way of attaching himself to them. Instead of this, they appear, in the main, sporadically; and are withdrawn or made harmless by other utterances. If this consideration be correct, the easiest explanation would be that the author was attached to the Gnostic ideas at an earlier date, and at the time he wrote had not succeeded in banishing them entirely from his mind, but to all intents and purposes had now passed beyond them to where he now stands.

CONCLUSION.

There still remain many important ideas in the Fourth Gospel that would repay discussion. But we cannot take them up here. In Part II. of this book we shall discuss them from a new point of view.

We trust that readers who have followed us so far will also give their attention to the briefer investigations to be undertaken there. Not only have we still to deal with the whole question, when and by whom the Fourth Gospel was really composed--which we shall deal with in connection with the same question as regards the three Epistles and the "Revelation" of Jn.--but we propose to add a few words as to the value of these remarkable writings for the time of their authors and for all times.

Whoever desires to know no more than this, whether the Fourth Gospel gives us correct knowledge of the Life of Jesus, might stop at this point. He would then throw the Gospel on one side like an instrument which for any definite purpose is useless. But a book is not a mere instrument. It is the work of some man who, if he does not dryly add one note to another without being really interested in his work, introduces into it, perhaps unconsciously, but to a more delicate mind unmistakably, a part of his own soul. And from what we have already said it should be clear that, in the case of the Fourth Evangelist, this was so to a quite specially high degree. The more we have so far found him to be wrong, when he differs from the Synoptics, the more anxious we become to read his soul, by finding out the ideas and needs by which he was actuated, and to search lovingly for what it is that exercises such undeniable power of attraction over even the strictest of his critics.

PART II - ORIGIN AND VALUE OF THE GOSPEL, EPISTLES, AND REVELATION OF JOHN

INTRODUCTION

AMONG the twelve Apostles of Jesus a prominent place is taken by John, son of Zebedee and brother of the first of the two Jameses who were included in the band of twelve disciples. Tradition tells us that five of the writings contained in the New Testament are by him: the Fourth Gospel, the three Epistles of John, and "Revelation." By the side, on the one hand, of the first three Gospels, and, on the other, of those Epistles which were either composed by the Apostle Paul or have been wrongly ascribed to him, these writings form a group of their own in the New Testament which is quite as important as the others; and any one who proposes to examine them, must of course regard them all together.

CHAPTER I - AUTHOR OF THE FOURTH GOSPEL AND DATE AT WHICH IT WAS WRITTEN

WHAT has been said in Part I. contributes a very great deal towards the decision of the question, By whom and at what date was the Fourth Gospel composed? But it may be pointed out that all this was based solely on one definite view of the contents of the Gospel, and that besides this another is possible according to which the contents thoroughly deserve to be believed, have no connection with Gnosticism, or were directed against it--and so forth. Far more certain, we are told, are statements of men belonging to the oldest Christian times, who were still in a position to know the exact answer to our question. It will be seen whether they are more certain. In any case, we must hear what they are.

1. PAPIAS' TEACHER IN EPHESUS: JOHN THE ELDER.

Irenaeus, Bishop of Lyons, who wrote about 185, and nearly all the Christian writers of later date are unanimous in saying that the Fourth Gospel was composed by the Apostle John, who lived in Ephesus during about the last third of the first century and took a leading position in the eyes of all the Christian communities in the West of Asia Minor. Irenaeus, who must have been born about 140, in his early youth stayed at the house of the aged Bishop Polycarp of Smyrna in Asia Minor, who died in the year 156, and he often heard him speak of his teacher John. He adds that Papias also, the companion of Polycarp, who was afterwards bishop of Hierapolis in Asia Minor, was a hearer of the Apostle John.

But the latter statement is a mistake. Eusebius, the author of the first History of the Church (ob. 340) has in an earlier work simply repeated it from Irenaeus; in the History, however, which was written later, he has corrected it and, in proof of his right to do so, appeals to Papias own words in a work which, apart from this quotation, has been almost entirely lost. We shall give this memorable passage in order to show how a documentary statement may prove the incorrectness of extremely important ideas which have not been doubted by any one for centuries. Papias' book contained, as we know from its title, "Expositions of the Sayings of the Lord" Jesus. In the Introduction Eusebius found the following: "I shall not hesitate to gather up for you, with the expositions (belonging to the same), as well all that I once learnt well from the mouths of the elders and committed well to memory, I myself guaranteeing the truth of it. . . . But whenever any one came who had enjoyed intercourse with the elders, I inquired (firstly) about the sayings of the Elders, (as to) what Andrew or Peter said, or what Philip or what Thomas or James or what John or Matthew or any other of the disciples of the Lord (said), and (secondly) what Aristion and John the Elder, the disciples of the Lord, say."

Quite a number of important inferences may be drawn from this. (1) Papias gathered his information partly from the persons whom he calls "the Elders," partly from their disciples. (2) The Greek word which we render "the Elders" is presbyter. We cannot use this Greek word itself, because it would be understood to mean, as it does still in the Reformed Churches, leaders of a Christian community. But such an office is no guarantee that its holder could give what Papias needed--reliable memoranda of the Life of Jesus based as far as possible on personal observation; such a guarantee could only be given by persons of great age. Papias was born about 70; even if he began to collect his information at twenty years of age, the people who could tell him anything which they had learned by experience from their association with Jesus--that is to say, about the year 30--must have been already well advanced in years. (3) Jesus twelve apostles would have been the proper people to have spoken to, but Papias did not speak to any of these. It would really be very unnatural for him to wish on his own part to guarantee for the first time the truth of what he had heard from such all-important persons. But, besides this, he expressly tells us that he inquired about the sayings of the Elders from companions of the Elders--inquired as to what Andrew and the six others first mentioned said, and what Aristion and John the Elder say. It is clear that only these two were still alive when Papias gathered his information, and that those who are mentioned before them were no longer living. But these are actually seven of Jesus twelve Apostles; and there can be no idea of his having spoken personally to any of the five others, since he would not in that case under any consideration have failed to mention it. (4) We must therefore distinguish four stages: the twelve Apostles whom Papias no longer knew, the elders whom he still knew, their disciples, and lastly Papias himself. (5) Papias distinguishes between two persons with the name John: the Apostle and the person whom he calls "John, the Elder." Both belong to the "disciples of the Lord," but each in a different sense. The Apostle was a constant disciple of Jesus; the other was not; in fact, it may be that he only heard Jesus a few times in his early youth. When the first century came to an end, and the persons who could boast of a personal acquaintance with Jesus died out, it became easier for the title of honour, "disciple of the Lord," to be applied to one who, strictly speaking, little deserved it. (6) Papias may very well have known this second John. This need not be doubted on the ground that he inquired about his sayings of other persons; this only became necessary when he himself could no longer speak to him, either because he was living in a remote place or because he had died. In all probability Papias wrote his work between 140 and 160. At that time the John who had seen Jesus could certainly no longer be living; he may very well have lived during Papias youth.

We must assume with the greater certainty that Papias really knew him, because Irenaeus says that Papias was a hearer of the Apostle John, and yet, according to his own statements, he no longer knew the Apostle. Here then we have the confusion of which Irenaeus was guilty: Papias certainly had a John as his teacher; this, however, was not the Apostle, but John the Elder.

2. POLYCARP'S TEACHER IN EPHESUS: JOHN THE ELDER.

The confusion might appear harmless. It affects Papias merely; but the man with whom we are concerned, who told the young Irenaeus about his former teacher, the Apostle John, was Polycarp. But why does Irenaeus call Papias a companion of Polycarp, unless it be because both of them in their early youth had the same teacher? Both lived in Asia Minor, and when they were young there was only one John in Asia Minor. It was left for a Christian writer in the third century to note that there were statements about both John the Apostle and John the Elder which indicated Ephesus as their dwelling-place; and because he knew of no other way of adjusting these, he was obliged to think that the two men lived there simultaneously. But no one belonging to the earlier period has any knowledge of this, and it is clear from our records, every one of which knows only of one head of the Christian Church in Asia Minor, that there was no room for the two men at the same time. Irenaeus must therefore have been as much mistaken about Polycarp's teacher as about the teacher of Papias; and Polycarp was the disciple of John the Elder, not of the Apostle.

3. THE APOSTLE JOHN NOT IN EPHESUS.

Another thing that lends the strongest support to this conclusion is the fact that none of the Christian writers before Irenaeus knows anything of a stay of the Apostle John in Asia Minor; and yet this same John, who on the occasion of the meeting of Paul with the original apostles at Jerusalem (Gal. ii. 1-10 and Acts xv.) appears by the side of Peter and James (the brother of Jesus) as one of the three pillars of the first community, is one of the most important persons in primitive Christianity.

We will point to one fact only. When Paul took fare well of those who presided over the community at Ephesus (Acts xx. 29), he prophesied that after his departure fierce wolves would force a way in and would not spare the flock. This farewell address was not actually so delivered by Paul, but was composed by the author of the Acts (between about 105 and 130) in accordance with his own ideas a liberty which every ancient historian took with the speeches of his heroes, and which no one thought wrong, seeing that the most famous of the Greek historians, Thucydides (about 400 B.C.), expressly declares (I. xxii. 1) that he followed this plan in his work because it would have been an impossibility to have reported the exact words of the speeches as delivered. But how could the author of the Acts of the Apostles, who was as full of a feeling of veneration for the original apostles as he was for Paul, have introduced into Paul's speech so unfriendly an utterance about his successors, if he had any idea that the most important and influential of these was the Apostle John? But, further, if it be supposed that Paul actually made the utterance, without, of course, having any idea of the person of his successor, how could the author incorporate it in his book, and thus seriously impede his own main purpose--that of showing the unanimity subsisting between Paul and the original disciples--instead of quietly ignoring it, as he does so much that is unfavourable to the original apostles and their adherents (so we learn from the Epistles of Paul; e.g., Gal. ii. 11-21; i. 6 f.; vi. 12 f.)?

4. CONFUSION OF THE TWO JOHNS.

But, as a boy, Irenaeus often heard Polycarp himself speak of his teacher John; how, then, can a mistake have been possible as to which John was meant? Well, the riddle explains itself. Both Johns were "disciples of the Lord." As a rule, Polycarp only needed to say, "my teacher John, the disciple of the Lord," and the young Irenaeus only too easily made the mistake of supposing that he meant the apostle, who was perhaps the only John of whom he had so far heard. In fact, Irenaeus himself says regularly in his book, when he means the Apostle John, as we have just conjectured that Polycarp did, "the disciple of the Lord," whereas for Paul he always uses the expression "Apostle."

Once a mistake of the kind had arisen, the statement would be believed only too readily. The community in a city thought it a great honour to have been founded by an apostle, or led by one for some time. In the second century the idea grew up that the bishop of a community must have been consecrated to his office through the laying-on of hands either by an apostle or by a bishop who had received his own consecration at the hands of an apostle. It was thought that the capacity to fill the office of bishop, the so-called "charisma of office," could be transferred from one person to another only through this laying-on of hands by a consecrated person, and the first of such a series must always be an apostle. Thus it was naturally of the greatest importance to be able to show that in the past an apostle himself laboured in the community. Every one believed that he attended to the consecration of his successor; otherwise doubts might arise as to whether a bishop was properly consecrated.

We must not suppose that the confusion by which Ephesus was given an apostle, instead of one who was not an apostle, as the leader of the community is an isolated case. In the Acts of the Apostles (vi. 5) we find included among the seven almoners of the community at Jerusalem a Philip who, according to xxi. 8 f., was an evangelist, that is to say, a missionary, and had four daughters who were endowed with the gift of prophecy. At the end of the second century this same Philip was identified with Philip the Apostle. Thus Hierapolis, where he is supposed to have stayed at the end of his life, was provided with an apostle as the head of the community.

5. EARLY DEATH OF THE APOSTLE JOHN (IN PALESTINE).

Where then, if it was not he but John the Elder who led the Church of Asia Minor in Ephesus, did John the Apostle live, and why are we not told another word about his fate since the meeting in Jerusalem we have mentioned (Gal. ii. 1-10)? As regards this also Papias gives us information, but this time in another sentence of his book which became known to scholars only a few years ago: "John, the man of God, and his brother James were killed by Jews." We are also told this about James in the Acts of the Apostles (xii. 2); he was executed at Jerusalem in the year 44 by Herod Agrippa I. Of the John who was head of the Church in Ephesus we know the contrary: there is no other record but this, that he died a natural death at a great age. But there is really no contradiction here, if we realise that this was a different John from John the Apostle. Besides, in Ephesus, where the Jews were closely watched by a foreign power, they would hardly have dared to lay hands on the bishop of the Christian community. It would be quite different if the Apostle John, whom, as we learn from the story of Papias, they killed, lived in Pales tine. And as a matter of fact at the meeting with Paul (about 52) mentioned above, he, as well as Peter and James (the brother of Jesus), declared this intention: they wished to go as missionaries to the Jews (Gal. ii. 9).

Only, we must beware of misunderstanding the words of Papias as if he meant that John and his brother James were killed at the same time. If that were so, it would certainly be impossible to understand why only the death of James is reported in the Acts of the Apostles. But besides this, the idea that they died together does not suit the words of Papias. No one has ever said that John the Baptist was killed by Jews; every one says, by Herod Antipas (Mk. vi. 17-29). Similarly, if Papias had meant to say that the two brothers had perished at the same time and on the same pretext he would have said: they were killed by Herod Agrippa 1. When he says, instead of this, "by Jews," it is most natural to suppose that John at least perished in such a way that no such notable person as a prince could be referred to as the author of his death. The sooner we can suppose the death of John to have taken place after the year 52, the easier it is to understand, on the one hand, why we do not hear more of his work, and, on the other, how the John in Ephesus, alongside of him, could become so prominent that in the end he was confused with him.

6. RESULT AS FAR AS THE FOURTH GOSPEL IS CONCERNED.

The result as far as the Fourth Gospel is concerned is as follows. The earlier the apostle died, the less easy it is to think that he wrote the Gospel. It is almost universally admitted that the first three Gospels were completed before the fourth; and of these the third at least was not composed until after the destruction of Jerusalem in the year 70 (provisionally we confine ourselves to a statement the truth of which is recognised almost on all hands). But even if we do not suppose that the Apostle died early, he cannot be regarded as the author of the Gospel because, as we have seen, he did not live in Ephesus. The Christian writers who look upon him as the author do not say that the Apostle composed it, no matter where he lived, but they say, "the John who was head of the Church of Asia Minor wrote it," so that the Apostle may be held to be the author of the Gospel only if we can think of him as living in Ephesus. If he lived elsewhere, we cannot say that these writers regarded him as the author; for by the John who in their opinion wrote the Gospel, they always mean the John in Ephesus. Accordingly, their "testimony" to the effect that the Apostle was the author is evidence, rather, that some one else was the author.

7. THE TESTIMONY OP THE BELOVED DISCIPLE.

But what about the author's own testimony? Does he not himself say that he is the Apostle? This is surely a curious question! When a matter is to be decided in other fields--when, for instance, the origin of extra-canonical books is in question, or a trial is being held--scant consideration indeed is paid to the personal testimony of the person involved; but here forsooth this is to be decisive, and all arguments against it, however plausible, are to be ignored. This is to take for granted--is it not?--what, strictly speaking, should first be proved, that a person whose book has been included in the Bible cannot have said anything incorrect.

But let us hear what this testimony is. The author nowhere refers to the name John as being his own. The superscription "Gospel according to John" is not due to him, but was first added when several Gospels were put together in one book. [7] Neither, however, does he ever refer to the Apostle John by this name. But he has him in mind when he says that after the arrest of Jesus, "Simon Peter and another disciple "followed him to the Palace of the High Priest (xviii. 15), and that "Peter and the other disciple "went to the grave of Jesus (xx. 1-10). Here he writes more fully (xx. 2), "Simon Peter, and that other disciple whom Jesus loved," and the simple description, "one of the disciples whom Jesus loved," is found already in xiii. 23, where it is said that at Jesus' last supper he "reclined in Jesus bosom"; finally, we learn from xix. 26, that "the disciple whom he loved" stood with Jesus mother at the foot of the cross.

In this circumlocution we see, it is said, the delicate and sensitive way in which the Apostle John hinted that he was the author of the Gospel, without expressly saying so. In reality, if he did this, he would have shown himself to be an incredibly presumptuous person. Jesus surely loved all his disciples! If the author had said of himself, "the disciple whom Jesus specially loved," we could not acquit him of presumption, even though this were really the case; but he says outright, "the disciple whom Jesus loved," as if he loved him alone. It is not really doing the Apostle any honour to insist that he must have described himself in this way. On the other hand, it is quite easy to understand that one of his devoted admirers may have so described him. But if we examine further all that is told us about the beloved disciple--the story, in particular, of his race with Peter to the grave of Jesus is so incredible (p. 133 f.) that we cannot imagine it to have been committed to writing by an eyewitness. And so here again this "testimony" of the author to the effect that he is the Apostle becomes evidence, rather, that some one else was the author.

8. FURTHER WITNESS OF THE AUTHOR TO HIMSELF (Jn. xix. 35).

The most characteristic instance of the author testifying to himself--an instance in which there is a real idea of bearing testimony--is held to be that in xix. 34 f.: "one of the soldiers with a spear pierced his side (the side of the crucified Lord), and straightway there came out blood and water; and he that hath seen hath borne witness, and his witness is true, and he knoweth that he saith true, that ye also may believe." We must remember here that we were told in verse 26 that the beloved disciple stood at the foot of the cross; it is he therefore who is meant when reference is made to one who saw the flowing of blood and water. But is it he himself who pens the words?

Searching inquiries have been instituted as to whether, in speaking of himself in Greek, any one could say "he." But this is not the point. Once the Apostle had begun by saying, instead of "I," "he that hath seen," there was no other way to continue than by saying "he." So that the question is: When the writer says "he that hath seen," does he mean himself? This in itself would be quite possible, if he wished to avoid the use of "I." Throughout the whole description of his wars (58-48 B.C.), Julius Caesar has never said "I did this and that," but always "Caesar did this and that." But, if he wished to express himself similarly, it would have been far more correct for the Fourth Evangelist to say: "he that hath seen it, bears witness" (now, as he writes it down). The expression, "he hath borne witness" would be far more appropriate if the observer of what occurred told it orally and another person recorded it in writing afterwards. Yet according to Greek Syntax the expression might also mean: he wishes (hereby) to have testified; and in this case it is still possible that what we read in this passage was written down by the observer.

It is decisive here that blood and water cannot by any means have flowed separately from Jesus' wound so soon after his death (it was at most two hours, but probably much less; see p. 127). It is therefore doing no honour to the Apostle to insist that he is here bearing personal testimony. On the other hand, we can very well under stand a later writer, who had been orally assured that it really happened, noting it down in good faith.

We should add further, that in any case the flowing of water and blood has some deeper mysterious meaning. It was a common Christian belief that the blood of Jesus shed at his death was the means of bringing salvation to man kind. Now, the individual Christian can partake of the blood of Jesus in the Supper, and is reminded of the redemption which has through his blood been granted to men. And water is used in baptism for the purpose of initiating people into communion with those who have been redeemed by the death of Jesus. Accordingly, the idea that the two things which are necessary for the most important and holy of the Christian ceremonies came into being at the death of Jesus is an ingenious one. We can easily imagine that a preacher may have expressed the idea in a veiled form, just as was done, if we have conjectured rightly (p. 113 f.), in the case of the story of Lazarus, and that some one in the audience jumped to the conclusion that it might be recorded as an actual fact that blood and water flowed from Jesus wound.

9. NO DECEPTION IN WRITING UNDER PSEUDONYMS.

If what we have said indicates that it was not the Apostle, but another who wrote the passage which speaks of testifying to the blood and water, and at the same time wrote the whole Gospel, we do not of course know as yet whether he wishes to be regarded merely as the reporter of the testimony of a greater person, or whether he wishes it to appear that he himself is this greater person, this eye witness. Even one who at the outset does not hold the Biblical writers in particularly high esteem, will readily be inclined to find the second supposition unthinkable, be cause it would imply such an amount of dishonesty as there is no reason to ascribe to the Evangelist, whose style is simple and candid.

But, as regards this matter, people quite ignore the fact that in those days it was not considered wrong to compose a writing in the name of another person. Among the Greeks and Romans it was quite common for disciples to publish their works, not under their own name, but under that of their masters; and we can see in what light this was regarded, from the philosopher Iamblichus (about 300 A.D.), for example, who was one of the followers of Pythagoras. We know even at the present time of a list of sixty writings which have been fathered upon Pythagoras and other old masters amongst his successors; and Iamblichus expressly praises the later disciples of Pythagoras, because they have sacrificed their own fame and given all the glory to their masters.

As regards Christian writers, the story of the leader of a Church in Asia Minor, who published the history of Paul and Thecla in the second century under the name of the Apostle Paul, is specially instructive. When he was reproached for doing so, he replied that he did it out of love for Paul; and Tertullian, the Church writer and jurist at Carthage (about 200), who tells us about it, does not think of charging him with it as a sin, but only makes fun of him for his incapacity in the words: "as if his work could do anything to increase the fame of Paul." The man was deposed, not however because he had been guilty of anything that we should call a forgery, but because he said in his book that Thecla came forward to teach in public and baptized herself by jumping into a ditch filled with water in view of death by wild beasts in the Circus. Both things were contrary to the regulations of the Church (on the first see 1 Cor. xiv. 34, "Let the women keep silence in the churches"). They were not allowed; but there was no offence in the publication of a writing in the name of another person.

This way of looking at the matter makes it very easy for us to understand how so many of the books of the New Testament were composed in the name of Paul, of Peter, of James, &c. And strange as it may appear, we must thoroughly accustom ourselves to it. To show that this suggests itself even to a quite orthodox theologian, we will quote an utterance by Professor Kahnis of Leipzig, who died in 1888. "If the fifth book of Moses is not by Moses, it is by an impostor, says Dr. Hengstenberg. To whom does Dr. Hengstenberg say this? Every one who has been to a classical school knows that there are a great number of writings in classical literature which are ascribed to persons with famous names, and that specialists do not think there was any deception in the practice." As regards the Second Epistle of Peter, even very conservative theologians now admit that it was written one hundred and twenty or more years after Jesus' death, although, in speaking of Jesus transfiguration, its author assures us, quite as if he were the Apostle Peter (i. 18): "and this voice we ourselves heard come out of heaven, when we were with him on the holy mount." Why then should the same thing not have happened in the case of the Fourth Gospel?

Thus we need not shrink from crediting the author of the Fourth Gospel with the wish to have his book regarded as the work of the Apostle himself. We have, however, no absolutely definite ground for saying so. The matter remains obscure. And perhaps it was meant to remain obscure. The testimony we have been examining could, as a matter of fact, hardly have been framed in a more enigmatic way than in the terms, "and his witness is true, and he knoweth that he saith true." It is possible therefore that the author, though he did not wish to say expressly that his book was the work of the Apostle, had no objection to people believing so. Even when he says in i. 14 "the Logos became flesh . . . and we beheld his glory", it is not certain whether he means with our bodily eyes (which, in view of what we have said above, would not need to be regarded as a fraudulent assertion), or whether he wishes to imply that those who were not privileged to do this saw his glory with their spiritual vision by means of the stories of Jesus' life, and of the blessings which proceeded from him even after his death.

10. CHAPTER XXI AN APPENDIX FROM ANOTHER PEN.

We could not, it is true, seriously impute this obscurity to him, if the twenty-first chapter were due to the same author. But this is not the case. For the same concepts quite different words are used here from those found in the first twenty chapters. The appearance of the risen Lord in chapter xxi. (14) is said to be the third; but three others have already been mentioned in chapter xx. Peter is a fisher, as in the Synoptics (Mk. i. 16), whereas Jn. (i. 35-41) knows him only as a disciple of the Baptist. But, most important of all, in chapter xxi. Peter appears in a much more favoured light than before; he even receives the commission to feed Jesus sheep, that is to say, to guide the Church, and is told that he is likely to have the honour of dying a martyr's death. The beloved disciple, on the other hand, who has always taken precedence of him in chapters i.-xx. (xiii. 24; xviii. 16; xix. 26; xx. 2-10), in chapter xxi. (22-24) has to content himself with a humbler role: he is promised a long life, and is given the task of writing the Gospel. This striking recognition of Peter is in all likelihood due to the fact that offence had been taken because in chapters i.-xx. he was made subordinate to the beloved disciple. Peter had already won high esteem in the Christian Church, especially at Rome, and the friends of the author of the Gospel must have feared, or, as we shall see shortly, must have found, that for this reason the book was gaining slight recognition. One of them therefore decided to reckon with these circumstances by adding an appendix.

And because the Gospel had gained such slight recognition, he took occasion at the same time, in the appendix which he added, to assure its readers once more that the author was the famous John. This he does (xxi. 24) with more clearness and emphasis than the author himself: "this (that is to say, the long-lived beloved disciple) is the disciple which beareth witness of these things, and wrote these things: and we know that his witness is true." We? Who? Here we have a hint that the author of the appendix has perhaps been commissioned by a whole number of the party of the Evangelist to write, or at least writes to voice their sentiments and to promote the idea that the Gospel was composed by the beloved disciple and for that reason deserves to be trusted absolutely. But his very zeal has been the means of discrediting him in the eyes of a serious critic. A witness, whose evidence must itself be witnessed to in turn, cannot seem a very trustworthy person.

11. THE REAL PICTURE OF JOHN THE APOSTLE.

After all these "witnesses" on the part of badly informed writers, of the author himself and of his friends who have intervened on his behalf, it is at length time to seek for some point from which we can learn better who wrote the Fourth Gospel. What information have we then in the New Testament about the Apostle John which is really reliable? We must not of course turn to the Fourth Gospel for our answer. The most certain thing is the record of Paul, that John was one of the three pillars of the Community in Jerusalem, and wished to confine his missionary activity to the Jews (see pp. 174 and 177), the reason being no doubt that, if he held intercourse with the Gentiles, he would violate the Old Testament commandments about foods, cleanness, &c., which he thought ought still to be observed. This does not harmonise well with the fact that in the Fourth Gospel Jesus calls the Law a "Law of the Jews" and feels that he is quite superior to it. Further, the whole view of the world, familiar as it is with the ideas of the greatest Greek thinkers, and the boldness with which, following the example of Gnosticism, all that is traditional is swept away--all this, which we have found in the Gospel, suits no one so little as this man who had remained stationary and simply persisted in holding the standpoint of the Old Testament. Add to this that according to Mk. i. 19 he was a fisherman, and according to Acts iv. 13 a man without learning and culture. Nor is this altered by the fact that he, with his brother James and with Peter, was one of the most intimate companions of Jesus in the circle of the twelve disciples (Mk. v. 37; ix. 2; xiv. 33).

12. MISTAKES AS TO THE CONDITION OF THINGS IN PALESTINE.

One who writes under an assumed name often betrays himself by having false ideas of the places or institutions of the country in which he claims to be living. As far as places are concerned, it cannot be shown with success that Jn. does this. But, as regards institutions, he has been led to make as great a mistake as it is possible to imagine. By telling us twice (xi. 49, 51, and xviii. 13) that Caiaphas was "high priest that year" he assumes that the office changed hands every year. As a matter of fact, the high priest held the office for life, and, although it happened not infrequently that one was deposed, there was never any question of a yearly vacation of office. This of course is a fact which would have been as well known to a contemporary of Jesus in Palestine, as the fact that the office of Emperor is hereditary is to a German of to-day. In face of a mistake on such a matter, how can we attach importance to the knowledge of places in the country, which could easily be acquired even one hundred years after the events with which they are associated?

13. JOHN THE ELDER NOT THE WRITER OF THE FOURTH GOSPEL.

May we therefore speak of John the Elder in Ephesus as the author of the Fourth Gospel? Support for this might, as a matter of fact, be found in the consideration that Irenaeus and his successors virtually supposed this, even though they believed that this John in Ephesus was the Apostle. But the assumption will not bear closer examination. If he was a disciple of Jesus, and consequently a man whose home was in Palestine, he ought to have known more about the tenure of the high-priest's office. But, above all, his standpoint was hardly less Jewish-Christian than that of the Apostle. In fact when Polycarp (see p. 173), who was a former disciple of his, visited Rome towards the end of his life (154 or 155), and found that Easter was fixed at a quite different time (the time at which we still fix it) from that of Asia Minor, where he lived, he appealed to the practice of John (and others). In Asia Minor what, according to the Jewish Calendar, was always the 14th Nisan was duly celebrated, not in memory of the death of Jesus--as the Fourth Gospel would require (p. 118)--but of the institution of the Supper a practice which conflicts with the Fourth Gospel, and is, as a matter of fact, supported by a special appeal to Mt. The John who shared this practice as leader of the Church of Asia Minor cannot have written the Fourth Gospel. Moreover, this would be equally true of John the Apostle if he had been the leader of the Church of Asia Minor.

14. WHAT KIND OP PERSON WAS THE FOURTH EVANGELIST?

If this means that we must give up the idea of naming some well-known person as the author, we are, nevertheless, very well able to form a clear idea of the writer of the Fourth Gospel. In seeking to do so, we have come back, after making a long circuit, to our starting-point, for we have to consult the Gospel itself. To have been able to write such a book, the author must have been one of the leading spirits of his age. He was familiar with the best that the Greek mind and the religions of the whole world known to people of those days had produced. His own mind was liberal enough to soar to the realm of these ideas, and to refuse to allow itself to be cramped by anything traditional. He knew how to gather into a common reservoir all the streams of thought that flowed towards him from the most diverse sources. His great object was to use all for the glorification of Jesus as he conceived him. Even Gnosticism, the most dangerous movement of his time, was well known to him--so much so that he had made many of its ideas his own. But he recognised the danger in it and did all in his power to overcome it, without giving up anything in Gnosticism which was really lofty and emancipating.

His chief pattern was Philo, and he perhaps had some thing else in common with him in the fact that he was of Jewish extraction. If he had not been, he would hardly have attached so much importance to the fulfilment of Old Testament prophecies (see p. 128 f.), and would hardly have made Jesus say "salvation is of the Jews" (iv. 22). He cannot of course have received his wide culture in Palestine. Accordingly, we must seek his home outside of this country, and preferably in a great city which would gather up all the wisdom of the known world. Ephesus would suit the requirements admirably, and if the Gospel came into existence here, it would be very easy for it to be ascribed to a person who had taken a very prominent position in the city at an earlier date, John the Elder whether or not it was done in such a way that he was sup posed to be the Apostle. Ephesus will suggest itself again when we inquire into the origin of the "Revelation" of Jn.; and in itself it is rather likely that all the five writings which are supposed to have been composed by John the Apostle would have come into existence amongst the same circle of men of kindred spirit, and so in one and the same locality. But we cannot rely upon all these considerations, nor need we think it important to be able to say where the Gospel was written.

15. DATE AT WHICH THE FOURTH GOSPEL WAS COMPOSED.

More pressing is the question, When did it come into existence? And, as regards this, we must of course look once more for statements outside the Gospel. When were the first three Gospels written, which, by almost general agreement, were all known to the writer of the Fourth? If we may voice our own conviction, it would suffice to say that the Third Gospel cannot have come into existence until about the year 100, because the author was well acquainted with the writings of the Jewish historian Josephus who composed his chief work in the year 93 or 94. Others, who place the Gospel of Lk. (and so the Gospels of Mk. and Mt. also) earlier, think that, when this estimation is taken into consideration, the Gospel of Jn. may have been composed as early as about the year 100. But here again we have to remember that the Gnosticism with which the Fourth Evangelist is familiar, and which he vigorously opposes, did not force its way into the Christian communities until about the year 100. We learn this from Hegesippus, who wrote his "memorials" about the year 180, and as he was of a great age was still able to afford correct information on the matter. Jn., on the other hand, already had to do with a more developed form of Gnosticism (p. 205). Only, he does not seem to be acquainted with the forms which appeared after about the year 140.

16. THE APOSTLE IS NOT MENTIONED AS THE AUTHOR UNTIL AFTER THE YEAR 170.

The most important and decisive point is to know from what date we have reliable external evidence, as we say, concerning the Fourth Gospel; in other words, statements by writers which imply that they knew the book as the work of such and such an author, or at least that they wrote out passages from him, so that there can be no mistake that they really had the book lying before them. This, in fact, is the point on which those who claim that the Gospel was composed by John the Apostle have staked everything. Many of them have undertaken no less a task than to prove by such external testimony that the author ship has been placed so much beyond doubt that it is not permissible even to take into consideration the counter arguments drawn from other considerations, for instance from an examination of the Gospel itself.

Unfortunately it is quite impossible here to go into this point with all the thoroughness that is really required. If we thought of doing so, we should have to give verbatim an almost endless number of passages from all the writers of the second century, in order to enable the reader to decide whether or not they betray a knowledge of the Fourth Gospel. We should be obliged, further, in the case of all these writers to state when they wrote, or rather, since in most cases the matter is not certain, to make inquiry and try to fix the most likely date. Ten years earlier or later here mean a very great difference. Finally, we should be obliged to find out their habits: whether to a greater or less extent they incorporate in their works passages from other books; whether they are accustomed to do this exactly word for word or merely from memory; whether they state regularly from what book they draw, or simply write down the words without saying that they have borrowed them; whether they use books which we no longer possess. All this may be important when it is a question whether a passage in their writings which resembles one in the Fourth Gospel is taken from this or not. Instead of going into all these troublesome and wearisome questions, it must suffice here to state the results briefly, and to show by a few examples how they have been attained.

First then we have to establish the fact that before the year 170 no writer can be found who ascribes the Fourth Gospel to John the Apostle. As regards this matter, we must note further that the year 170 is the very earliest that can be specified, for the statement we have in mind that belongs to this time reads simply: as to the day of Jesus' death "the Gospels seem to be at variance." The name, therefore, of John the Apostle is not mentioned. But it is clear from the words that this writer (Claudius Apollinaris) puts the Fourth Gospel, which introduces the variance (for the first three are quite agreed; see p. 118 f.), on the same level as the others.

17. VALUE OF THESE "EXTERNAL EVIDENCES."

But if from this date it is almost generally regarded as the work of the Apostle, in order to be able to determine the value of this assertion, we must know in the first place the general idea which leading persons of the time had of the books of the New Testament.

On this point Irenaeus (about 185) is specially instructive. To prove that there are just four true Gospels (there were still many others in existence), he points to the fact that there are four quarters of the world and four winds; since, then, the Church is scattered over the whole earth and the Gospel constitutes its pillar and support and the spirit of its life, it is appropriate that the pillars which on all (four) sides blow upon it with the airs of imperishability should be four in number--in other words, the four Gospels. Such was the idea of so distinguished a person as Irenaeus; when it was a question of deciding whether the Fourth Gospel was composed by John the Apostle, he took his stand on the fact that the quarters of heaven and the chief winds are four in number. To understand how he could do this while speaking of the spirit of life, as well as of the winds, we must be aware that in Greek "wind "and "spirit "are represented by the same word (pneuma). So that by means of a play upon words, to sustain which he has further to think of pillars (i.e., the Gospels) as blowing, he is prepared to decide a question of such great importance. Surely we are justified in practically ignoring the proof which a person of this stamp brings forward to show that such and such a person was the author of a book in the New Testament.

But we will take a few more cases as tests of the care fulness of Irenaeus and those of his contemporaries who agreed with him in claiming that the Fourth Gospel was composed by John the Apostle; they will serve to test their critical powers as well. Irenaeus regards the James who is said in Acts xv. to have been present at the already-mentioned (p. 174) meeting with Paul as one of the three pillars of the Church at Jerusalem as that brother of John and personal disciple of Jesus whose execution has been recorded three chapters further back (xii. 2). In the Gospel of Lk. again he thinks that the discourses of the Apostle Paul concerning the Life of Jesus are committed to writing just as those of Peter are in the Gospel of Mk.--and this in spite of the fact that Paul never met Jesus, and continued to persecute the Christians even after Jesus' death. Dealing with the question of eternal happiness, Irenaeus is able to tell us that there will be vines with 10,000 stems, on each stem 10,000 branches, on each branch 10,000 shoots, on each shoot 10,000 clusters, on each cluster 10,000 berries, and that every berry will yield 900 to 1000 litres of wine. The most important point, however, is not the size of these vines, but Irenaeus statement, that Jesus himself prophesied this; the aged men whom he so often mentions had told him so, and had added that they had heard it from John the Apostle. And this Irenaeus believes, although he assures us so emphatically that this same person wrote the Fourth Gospel which makes Jesus appear so superior to all such expectations.

Clement of Alexandria, one of the most learned and most venerated teachers in the Church (about 200), quotes as an utterance of the Apostle Paul(!) the words, "take also the Greek books, read the Sibyl and see how it reveals one God and the future, and read Hystaspes, and you will find in them the Son of God described much more clearly." Hystaspes was the father of Darius, the Persian king who reigned from 521 to 485 B.C. The words of Clement give us some idea of the kind of fabrication that was put forth in his name. The credulous Clement also quotes the book of Zoroaster of Pamphylia in which he recorded after his resurrection all that had been taught him in the under world by the gods. The jurist Tertullian (about 200) is able to tell us that in the official account of Jesus condemnation which Pilate sent to the Emperor Tiberius, he mentioned, amongst other things, the eclipse of the sun at the time of Jesus' death, the guarding of the sepulchre, the resurrection of Jesus and his ascension, and that in his inmost convictions he was already a Christian. If Tertullian is not giving free rein to his imagination here, but has used some book ("Acts of Pilate"), we shall be glad to think that the author of it was a Christian.

But enough. We can see clearly the kind of people we have to deal with when the witnesses in support of the usual statements about the origin of the New Testament books are brought forward. Instead of insisting so emphatically that the fact that the Fourth Gospel was composed by John the Apostle is already borne witness to by Irenaeus, Tertullian, Clement of Alexandria and others, it ought in truth to be said that no one did so until they bore witness to it--or, rather, asserted it.

18. THE GOSPEL NOT USED BEFORE 140.

Of rather a different nature are the cases in which passages from the Fourth Gospel are merely cited without its being said who wrote them. As regards these, it can be shown that before the year 140 there is evidence of none to which we have strict right to appeal. Sayings and expressions which resemble some in this Gospel, are indeed found in Christian writings after about the year 100 not infrequently. But it is a very strange idea that this resemblance must always be accounted for by supposing that the writers had read the Fourth Gospel. Because the Gospel has first made us acquainted with these sayings and expressions, there is no need to suppose that the circum stances were the same as early as about the year 100. On the contrary, why may not the Fourth Evangelist have been acquainted with the writings in question? Or, to mention a suggestion which in many cases is more likely, the discourses of the travelling teachers of the times, of whom there were very many, may have given currency to a number of catchwords, phrases, and whole sentences, which became the common property of all more or less cultured Christians. No one could say where he first heard them. Any one who wrote a book made use of them without suspecting that the question from what other book he took them would ever be asked. It may be that the Fourth Evangelist availed himself of them, and stamped them with his own particular genius; and we of the present day may easily be misled into supposing that he must have been the first to coin them, and that all other writers who use them must have written subsequently.

It is particularly easy to think this when a whole sentence is in question, which contains in itself an independent and important thought. We have an example in Jn. xiv. 2, "in my Father's house (that is to say, in heaven) are many mansions." Those people of great age to whom Irenaeus often appeals, have handed down to him as a saying of Jesus the words, "in my Father's domains are many mansions." Besides this, we learn from Jn. alone (xiv. 2) that Jesus made this statement, and the conclusion is drawn that the "elders" also can only have become acquainted with it from the Gospel. And since they have been referred to by Irenaeus as people who speak not from a more recent age, but from their own recollection of the distant past, the Gospel must already have been in existence at a very early date. This is a typical example of the kind of proof it is not permissible to use. We refrain from reckoning with the possibility that Jesus may really have made the statement, and that the elders were just as likely as the Fourth Evangelist to have learned it orally. But in their case, as well as that of Jn., the belief may also have grown up erroneously that he made the statement. This assertion would then have been repeated, and so finally have found its way into the Fourth Gospel. It was certainly the kind of saying that was likely to have been passed on from mouth to mouth, for it contains the comforting assurance that after one's death one might look forward with certainty to finding a refuge in heaven. Another indication that the saying became current in this way may be found in the fact that the versions in Jn. and Irenaeus are not word for word identical.

19. USED WITHOUT RECOGNITION IN THE YEARS 140-170.

Most noteworthy are the writers between the specified years 140 and 170, who really cite passages from the Fourth Gospel, but do not say who composed it. The most important is Justin, who wrote about 152 and was subsequently martyred. From the Synoptics he introduces over one hundred passages, but from Jn. only three, and these are so far from following Jn.'s language exactly that in every case it can be thought that he took them from another book, and that the Fourth Evangelist may have done the same. We assume, however, that Justin took them from Jn.'s work. But why, then, are there so few, and why is nothing said about this work being the composition of a personal disciple of Jesus? Referring to the "Revelation" of Jn., he says positively that it was composed by the Apostle; but he says nothing about the Gospel. And yet he attaches so much importance to the "memorials of the Apostles and their companions," as he calls the Gospels; and shares with the Fourth the doctrine of the Logos. We can only understand this on one supposition: Justin did not consider the Fourth Gospel to be the work of the Apostle. In that case, it must in his age still have been quite new; otherwise it would long ago have won general recognition. Obviously Justin finds in it some passages which are beautiful and worth mentioning, but, compared with the rich use made of the Synoptics, he uses it with great caution, and almost with hesitation.

20. CONCLUSION AS TO THE "EXTERNAL EVIDENCES."

When therefore we sum up the results of our examination of the external evidence for the Fourth Gospel, we find that the lesson it teaches is the opposite of what those who believe that it was written by the Apostle think it ought to teach. Instead of proving that this was written very early, it proves that it was composed at a very late date. If the work in question were that of an obscure person, we can perhaps understand that it may have been in existence for decades without attracting attention or gaining recognition. But think of it! A work by the disciple whom Jesus loved! And, besides, a work containing disclosures of such paramount importance! It could not have failed to be greeted on its first appearance with the greatest joy, and to be greedily devoured; we could not fail to find an echo of it in all Christian writers. Instead of that, from the date at which it must have been published by the Apostle, that is to say, at latest from 90-100, until 140, there is not one certain instance of the use of the book; we do not find the Apostle recognised as the author until after 170, and in the meantime we do find it clearly realised that it was not by him. Indeed, we have to add further that after 160 or 170 it was positively stated by some who were good Churchmen, and later by the Presbyter Gaius in Rome at the beginning of the third century, to have been composed by a heretic. The result therefore of examining the external evidence means that we cannot place the origin of the Gospel earlier than very shortly before the first appearance of this evidence, and so very shortly before 140.

21. MENTION OF BAR COCHBA S INSURRECTION IN JN. v. 43 .

Let us now return to a consideration of the Gospel itself, and ask whether we cannot really get the best information as to the date at which it was composed in the same way that we have obtained it in considering the questions who was its author, and whether the work is reliable. Here then our attention is arrested by Jesus' words to the Jews in v. 43, "I am come in my Father's name, and ye receive me not: if another shall come in his own name, him ye will receive." In the year 132 Simon, having taken the name Bar Cochba, came forward, proclaimed himself the Messiah, and became among the Jews the leader of a fanatical rising against the Roman rule, with the result that in the year 135 the Jewish nation finally lost its in dependence. The Christians, as we can well understand, declared against the new Messiah from the first, and in consequence were fiercely persecuted so long as he retained any power. If the Fourth Evangelist had had experience of all this, may he not have thought that it would be under stood and would make an impression if he put into Jesus mouth a prophecy of these events? In that case he would have written between 132 and 140. If it had not been that for other reasons we have already been led to assign the composition of his book to about this date, we might not have had the boldness to appeal to this passage; but, such being the case, we seem to be really justified in doing so.

22. THE FOURTH GOSPEL NOT THE WORK OF SEVERAL AUTHORS.

We have reserved a question for discussion last, which, it might be thought, ought to have been dealt with first. Can it be that the Fourth Gospel is not by one and the same author? If not, whenever any assertion is made with regard to the author, it must of course be stated very care fully to what part it refers. But the question is not of serious importance. We have mentioned that the story of the woman taken in adultery (vii. 53-viii. 11) and chap. xxi. are later additions (pp. 39 and 186 f.; see also p. 209). But this does not make the least difference to our explanation of the Gospel as a whole.

The case would be altered, only if we were obliged to partition the first twenty chapters in large part between two or more authors. The attempt to do this as a rule rests upon the supposition that one half is due to a trust worthy historian and an eye-witness, the other to a badly informed contributor. In an earlier part of this volume (p. 110 f.), we have already realised how far such assumptions are from making anything contained in the Gospel really credible. But in conclusion we will try to show the contradictions in which people involve themselves when they make a division of the kind.

One of the most recent of these attempts explains that the eye-witness Peter, whose record Mk. preserves in his Gospel, tells us that on the last evening of Jesus' life he celebrated the Supper with his disciples; and the eye-witness John that he washed their feet. Peter therefore knew nothing of the washing, and John nothing of the Supper. The eye-witness Peter--we are told further as regards--Jesus' idea of the judgment of the world, preserved the record that it would begin for all men on one and the same day at the end of the world; the eye-witness John recorded that for those who believed in Jesus it would never take place (v. 24), and it is the badly informed contributor who has added the version in v. 28 f. which agrees with the statement of Peter. The eye-witness Peter, we are told, finally, left a record which suggests that .Jesus never betrayed that he was conscious of having lived a life with God in heaven before his earthly life; the eye-witness John is able to tell us that Jesus said "before Abraham was, I am," "Glorify thou me with thine own self with the glory which I had with thee before the world was" (viii. 58; xvii. 5); and he wrote in the Prologue the sentences in which Jesus is described as the Logos who was with God before the be ginning of the world. In face of such contradictions, it is really no use bringing forward passages here in which the context is said to have been interrupted by some intervention on the part of the contributor. We have already found out the carelessness of the Evangelist (pp. 76-78, 81-83) and it sufficiently explains the contradictions which appear in his book, even if no one else helped to compose it.

Footnote:

7. The words are "Gospel according to John," not "Gospel of John"; similarly, "Gospel according to Mt., according to Mk., according to Lk." But this does not mean that such a gospel was written by another man with the help of communications from the person specially named. The word "Gospel" in these cases means, rather, "Account of the Life of Jesus," and the superscription means therefore "the Gospel History as composed by Mt., Mk., Lk., or Jn."

CHAPTER II - THE FIRST EPISTLE OF JOHN

WHAT is known as the First Epistle of John, though in reality it is not in epistolary form at all but in that of a circular addressed to the whole of Christendom, is to all appearances inseparably connected with the Gospel. Often, as we read, we can hardly say whether we have the one or the other book open before us. And in fact the matter on which they differ from each other most clearly is one which, from another point of view, serves to bring them together again.

1. MAIN PURPOSE: TO OPPOSE THE GNOSTICS.

Whereas, for instance, the Gospel never says that it is opposing false teaching within the Christian fold (except in x. 1-10: see p. 135 f.), the Epistle says this most emphatically. But we found certain utterances in the Gospel aimed at very definite opponents, in other words, at the Gnostics (pp. 152-154, 160-163); and the first Epistle likewise opposes the Gnostics. We are told (ii. 4) that the author's opponents asserted that they knew God; and it was knowledge on which the Gnostics prided themselves. We know further the doctrine of the Stoics according to which the logos or rather the individual logoi were like seeds of corn scattered throughout the world (p. 142 f.), and out of these the things of the world arose. The Gnostics applied this idea to themselves, and claimed that they had in their own persons the divine seed. There is a hint of this idea in iii. 9; and in i. 8, 10 of the Gnostics assertion that this made them sinless.

As to Jesus, the opponents of the writer of the Epistle taught that he was not the Christ (ii. 22). And in this again we can recognise the claim of the Gnostics, that Jesus was only a man who for a time and in a loose way became one with the Christ who had come down from heaven. This is seen even more clearly in iv. 2 f.; they deny that Jesus Christ is come in the flesh, an utterance which is aimed at the same time at that other idea of the Gnostics--that he had merely a phantom body (pp. 150, 152). And in v. 6 that teaching of theirs is opposed, according to which the man who suffered on the cross was not really the redeemer, that is to say, the Christ, who had come down from heaven. The author says here that he came, that is to say, to save mankind, not only with water through his baptism but also with blood through his death.

But, further, in iii. 4, 10, ii. 4 the author declares against "every one that doeth sin" or "that keepeth not God's commandments," and by sin he means opposition to the injunction in iii. 3, that every one should purify himself. What he has in mind therefore is an unholy, unbridled life. Now, it is hardly possible that this reproach, which is made more than once and in the most varied forms, can apply to persons other than those who are opposed in other passages throughout the Epistle. And if this be so, the Gnostics with whom we have to deal here are not, like many others, especially in the first decades of the second century, people who adhered to the law of the Old Testament. We already have to do with a more developed form of Gnosticism.

2. AGREEMENT WITH GNOSTICISM.

But it is remarkable that the man who so decisively opposes Gnosticism agrees with it entirely on a strikingly large number of points. He also cannot but think that there are two kingdoms very sharply opposed to each other, the kingdom of God, and that of the world which is ruled by the devil (ii. 16; iii. 8, 10; iv. 4-6), or the kingdom of truth and that of lies (ii. 21) and this opposition extends to mankind as well, the one part being from God and the other from the world, which "lieth in the evil one," that is to say, is under the dominion of the devil (v. 19).

We found that there is the same kind of agreement with the Gnostics in the Gospel (pp. 158-160). But the Epistle goes a step farther. While the Gospel only occasionally suggests that knowledge is a valuable thing (xvii. 3), the Epistle emphasises, in a way that a Gnostic could not excel, that the author and his party themselves possess the knowledge of God or of the truth (ii. 13 f., 20 f., 27; iv. 7). Further, as to the Gnostics belief that they had in themselves the divine "seed," the author maintains again that it is really he and those who think with him who possess it as their own. And on this point he ventures to make the strongest statement found in his Epistle: "Whosoever is begotten of God doeth no sin" (iii. 9; v. 18). By these he means himself and his party. And this is said by the same person who just before (i. 8, 10) has reproached his opponents in these words: "If we say that we have no sin, we deceive ourselves, and the truth is not in us." Here we can see how great a spell the ideas of the Gnostics exercised upon men's minds.

3. NATURE OF THE OPPOSITION TO GNOSTICISM.

But we see at the same time the peculiar nature of the attack that is made upon them. Those who opposed them claimed as their own all that was valuable in the things the Gnostics prided themselves on, and denied it to the Gnostics. And upon what ground? If these Gnostics really lived the sinful kind of life they were reproached with, this would assuredly provide a certain amount of justification for arguing on these grounds against the truth of their teaching, on the principle "by their fruits ye shall know them" (Mt. vii. 16). But it is much to be feared that the opponents of the Gnostics painted their excesses in darker colours than was just; and it would also be reasonable to ask whether they had as much light on their own side as (in their view) there was of shade in that of their opponents. Unfortunately, we are obliged to say that the New Testament writers are too prone to disparage their opponents by attacking their morals, and often they do so in a way that is very unpleasant. In this matter the Epistles to Timothy and Titus (which were not composed by the Apostle Paul, but in the first half of the second century), the Epistle of Jude from the same period, and the Second Epistle of Peter (which was not written by the Apostle Peter any more than the first Epistle, but is the latest book in the New Testament, and was not written until after the middle of the second century) offend in a special degree. It is very possible that by employing this method of warfare, they show at the same time that they are incapable of overcoming their opponents with intellectual weapons. The author of the Epistle to the Colossians provides an honourable exception; and from this we can see at the same time that Gnostic views were not always and necessarily associated with immorality.

As regards the First Epistle of John, we must say that in its attack on its opponents, compared with the writings mentioned above, it has observed a certain moderation. In form at least it is written in a calm and measured style. We note that the author feels the necessity of convincing his readers of the truth of what he says. Laying so great stress on knowledge as he does, he cannot have failed to desire this. True, his argument does not take the form of giving real proofs; he simply gives expression to his own conviction; but the brevity and simplicity with which he does so makes it so effective that he could really hope to make an impression by it.

On what then, in the last resort, does he take his stand when he opposes the Gnostics? On the Confession of the Church. People must confess that Jesus Christ has come in the flesh that is to say, has appeared with a body consisting of flesh; otherwise they are not from God, but are Christ's enemies, and, in denying the son, they are at the same time denying God the Father as well (iv. 2 f.; ii. 22).

4. THE EPISTLE NOT BY THE AUTHOR OF THE GOSPEL.

After all that has been said so far, the Gospel and the first Epistle might very well seem to have been the work of the same person; but on a closer view it is clear that in all probability the two writings had different authors. A number of important expressions occur only in the Epistle which the author of the Gospel would have had opportunities of using as well had he been familiar with them. But, above all, the convictions to which the Epistle gives expression bring it nearer than the Gospel to the ordinary, simple faith of the Church.

Jesus second coming from heaven, at which he will bring eternal happiness, in ii. 28, as amongst primitive Christians in general, is expected to take place on a definite day as an objective event; on the other hand, when the Evangelist speaks of a second coming of Jesus after his death, he does so only in the sense that it will be identical with the coming of the Holy Spirit into the hearts of believers, which of course happens at very different times (xiv. 16-18, 26-28). The Epistle follows the old idea closely in expecting that on that great day in the future all men will rise from the dead and come before the bar of judgment (iii. 2; iv. 17). In the Gospel this idea is found only in particular passages, for example in v. 28 f., or in a clause which is perhaps disturbing, or at least can always be dispensed with, "and I will raise him up at the last day," vi. 40, 44, 54, 39 (on this account perhaps added by another person, in order to make the book more acceptable to simple believers); but his principal idea on this point is that eternal life begins even in this world as soon as a man believes in Jesus, and that such a one will never come into judgment (v. 24). To the writer of the Epistle the most important redemptive act of Jesus seems to be his death (i. 7; ii. 2; iv. 10), as was generally thought since the time of the Apostle Paul; the Gospel gives expression to this belief only in i. 29, 36, and perhaps in xi. 50-52; xvii. 19 b, and assumes everywhere else that Jesus brought redemption by coming amongst men and bringing them that true knowledge which leads to believing in him. In the division which is made between God and the world, the Epistle does not go so far as the Gospel. The Evangelist's most significant train of thought is to the effect that God does not give his gifts directly to men, but to Jesus. Jesus is the first to bestow them upon men (xv. 9 f.); none can come to the Father save through him (xiv. 6). There are not wanting in the Gospel, as we have indicated already (p. 161), sayings which represent the idea, assumed throughout the Epistle (ii. 24; iii. 24; iv. 12 f., 15 f.), that men also can commune directly with God. But the difference is perceptible all the same. Finally, in place of the designation "Logos," the Epistle (i. 1) has "the Word of Life," by which one cannot perceive that Jesus is a Being who bears the name Logos and is well known from Greek Philosophy.

It is indeed permissible to think that one and the same person might have expressed himself differently in two works. But the facts of the case are certainly more easily understood if we suppose that we have to do with two different authors; and since, moreover, the Evangelist cannot have been John the Apostle, it is no use insisting that the author of the Epistle can have been no other than he.

5. DATE OF COMPOSITION.

But when was the Epistle written? Since it represents the simpler and earlier form of the Christian faith, it is natural to think it older than the Gospel. But the contrary may also have been the case; and there are many other writers who have not followed the Gospel of John, when it diverges from the original teaching, but have betaken themselves to this. We must therefore look for another means of deciding the question. Let me quote here ii. 12-14: "I write unto you, my little children, because your sins are forgiven you for his name's sake. I write unto you, fathers, because ye know him which is from the beginning. I write unto you, young men, because ye have overcome the evil one. I have written unto you, little children, because ye know the Father. I have written unto you, fathers, because ye know him which is from the beginning. I have written unto you, young men, because ye are strong, and the word of God abideth in you, and ye have overcome the evil one." This can hardly be understood to mean anything else than that the author wishes to inform his readers that what he now writes is essentially the same as he has already written to them once before. And thus it is very natural to suppose that he suggests that he had done this in the Gospel. With this the external evidence would agree; the Epistle, like the Gospel, is not used by Christian writers until after the year 140, and when it is first used there is no mention of the author's name.

6. SECONDARY PURPOSE: RECOMMENDATION OF THE FOURTH GOSPEL.

We must now devote a few more words to the purpose of the Epistle. We have hitherto explained that the author is opposing the Gnostics, but if what we have just said be correct, this does not exhaust the matter; another purpose is to repeat in another form what is contained in the Gospel and so to confirm it. Is there any connection between this and the fact that in the earliest days after its publication it gained so little recognition (p. 199 f.)? In that case, the purpose of the Epistle would be the same as that which induced some one, as we have already found (p. 186 f.), to add the twenty-first chapter to the Gospel. And just as in the addition to the Gospel the ruling idea was to satisfy the requirement that the account of Peter should be more favourable, sq in the present case the work was carried out in such a way as to avoid those statements in the Gospel which differed too much from the ordinary faith of the Church. Here we may again wonder whether this may not have been done by the author of the Gospel himself, and whether he may not have written in this way, to set aside his original views of set purpose. But it is easier to suppose that one who belonged to the circle of his followers wrote it to give expression to his own view of the matter.

We should have to assume at the same time that he wished to be taken for the Evangelist. But, according to the ideas of the time, there would be as little harm in this as there was in the other case where the Evangelist (perhaps) wished to be taken for John the Apostle (pp. 183-185). We must not therefore regard it as being in the slightest degree deceitful when we are told at the beginning of his circular: "that which was from the beginning, that which we have heard, that which we have seen with our eyes, that which we beheld and our hands handled, concerning the Word of Life (that is to say, concerning Jesus) . . . declare we unto you also." By taking up the pen in the name of the Evangelist, and yet writing in a rather different sense, the author served the great purpose of gaining recognition in the Church for the precious thoughts contained in the Fourth Gospel, knowing as he did how to remove all that was offensive; and it is quite possible that he helped in a real sense to achieve this purpose. He did not, however, fulfil in any way his opening promise (i. 1). There is not the least trace in his Epistle of anything that only an eye-witness of the Life of Jesus could know.

CHAPTER III - THE SECOND AND THIRD EPISTLES OF JOHN

THE agreement which we have noticed in the mode of expression and the thought of the Fourth Gospel and the First Epistle, is much less pronounced when we turn to the Second Epistle, and disappears even more in the Third. On the other hand, these two Epistles supplement the First from a new point of view.

1. PURPOSE OP THE TWO EPISTLES.

If we take note of what is most peculiar in them, we cannot help seeing that their main purpose is to insist that with certain members of the Christian Church communion must be ended. We read in 2 Jn. 10 f.: "If any one cometh unto you, and bringeth not this (the right) teaching, receive him not into your house and give him no greeting: for he that giveth him greeting partaketh in his evil works." Here the Gnostics are intended who are called in verse 9 people who "go onward."

In the Third Epistle the opposition to these is less perceptible; there was less opportunity, for the occasion for this Epistle was provided by disputes between the author and a certain Diotrephes as to the authoritative influence in the community. "I wrote somewhat unto the Church; but Diotrephes, who loveth to have the pre-eminence among them, receiveth us not . . . neither doth he himself receive the brethren, and them that would he forbiddeth, and casteth them out of the Church" (3 Jn. 9 f.). These brethren are therefore travelling Christians, who belong to the party of the author. The idea of the Epistle is to request Gaius, to whom it is addressed, to receive them kindly. The author claims to have an influence extending beyond his own dwelling-place. The Demetrius who is mentioned at the end of the Epistle, and of whom it is expressly stated that he "hath the witness of all men," may well have conveyed it himself.

2. ADDRESS OP THE TWO EPISTLES.

The Third Epistle, then, is addressed to a particular person. At first sight, this seems to be so with the Second Epistle as well, when we read, "the elder unto the elect lady and her children." But who is the lady? The last sentence of the Epistle runs: "The children of thine elect sister salute thee." Does the author actually write from the house of the sister of the recipient? And what does verse 4 mean? "I rejoice greatly that I have found certain of thy children walking in truth." Only certain? Was there not greater cause to express sorrow for the others? In short, the "lady" is not a particular woman; she is a community. We learn from Ephes. v. 31 f.; Rev. xix. 7, that the community was thought of as the bride of Christ who had been exalted to heaven, just as in the Old Testament the people of Israel is the bride of God. Since Christ is called "the Lord," the community might be called "the lady." It deserves to be called "elect" because it consists of all the chosen. Its children are of course the members of the community.

We need not stop to think, as regards this matter, that a community had been shown to be meant instead of what appeared at first sight to be one woman. Where should we have to look for it? There is no clue to anything of the kind. Any community, therefore, might suppose that it was greeted by that other community in which the author was staying. This means that the Epistle was meant for the whole church, and its contents suit this idea quite well. For a secondary purpose of the Epistle is found in the fact that the author wishes to warn people in quite a general way against the Gnostics and to emphasise the correct teaching about Jesus (2 Jn. 7-9). In this respect it falls into line with the first Epistle.

3. AUTHOR OF THE TWO EPISTLES AND DATE OF COMPOSITION.

While the Second Epistle insists, not only on opposition to, but on the expulsion of the Gnostics, it goes beyond the First, and so might with the Third seem to be later. Unfortunately we have no definite points from which to start in order to determine the date at which both were written. Yet, on the other hand, there is another fact which leads us to suppose that they preceded the Gospel and the First Epistle.

The author of both Epistles, that is to say, calls himself simply, "the elder." How it could be thought that, in spite of this clear description, he was the Apostle, is really difficult to explain. If we cannot say for certain who is meant by "the elder," yet it is clear that the Apostle would not have described himself in this way. When we read in v. 1 of the First Epistle of Peter (which, besides, is not by Peter, but was written at the beginning of the persecution of the Christians in Asia Minor in the year 112; see iv. 12, 15 f.), that Peter is addressing the elders of the community, and for this special reason calls himself their fellow elder we have something quite different. But, besides this, we know of one quite famous person who is continually called "the elder"; this is John "the Elder," head of the Church in Asia Minor. The use of his special name "the elder" may very well have been so widespread that his real name John was omitted.

Was he the writer of the Epistles? If the Gnostics did not succeed in gaining a following in the Christian communities until about the year 100 (p. 192), a considerable period of time must have elapsed before people would take measures to exclude them so harshly from communion. For many decades they regarded themselves as members of the Church, and, though they were opposed by other teachers in it, they were treated everywhere with toleration, A personal disciple of Jesus, such as John the Elder was, cannot have lived to see the time when they were excluded from communion.

Another person in his circle, who is not known to us, may have had the same title, and in course of time have come to be known solely by this name, "the Elder." But in view of the close relationship between, at least, the Second Epistle on the one hand and the First and the Gospel on the other, it is very likely that the author is supposed to be that John the Elder whom Irenaeus and the other Christian writers had in mind, even though they mentioned the Apostle as the writer of the Gospel and the First Epistle. Only, in that case, the two small Epistles would have been composed merely in the name of John the Elder, just as the First Epistle and (perhaps) the Gospel are represented as being works of John the Apostle.

And this would be the reason for supposing these two to be the earlier of the four writings in question. On this assumption, we shall have to think that in one particular place, Ephesus perhaps, there was a whole number of persons of like mind who were filled with a feeling of veneration for John the Elder, once head of this community, and at the same time were anxious, by writing books, to make their ideas current in the Church. Even if these ideas had ceased to be quite identical with those of their former Master, it was most natural for them to publish their first writings in his name. But perhaps they were made to realise that his reputation had not extended beyond the immediate circle in which he had once worked. In order, therefore, to make a greater impression, when they thought of publishing new works, such as the Gospel and the First Epistle, they felt obliged to choose a person who ranked still higher and publish them in his name; this person was John the Apostle. In this way the two small Epistles, in spite of the fact that their range is restricted, would contribute not a little towards giving us a very interesting and instructive glimpse of a whole series of events and struggles, which the idea that arose later, that their author was John the Apostle, to all intents and purposes served to overcloud completely.

CHAPTER IV - THE "REVELATION" OF JOHN

1. VARIOUS INTERPRETATIONS.

THE last book of the New Testament is called "Revelation" (Gk. Apokalypsis) of Jesus Christ, but after we have pored over the books--far more than a thousand--which have been written in the past years to explain it, it must appear so obscure that the seven seals which are mentioned in the book (chapters v. f.; viii. 1) as closing over the fate of humanity and being loosened one after another, must seem to clasp the book itself firmly together and to refuse to be broken.

It has been supposed to prophesy the whole history of the Church and even of the world, in each case of course down to the lifetime of the expositor, and nearly always in a different way. In the beast described in xiii. 1-10; xvii. 7-18, people have recognised emperor after emperor, pope after pope, one leader after another of the Vandals, Muhammedans, and Turks, as well as Luther, Napoleon I., Napoleon III., and the French General Boulanger (1891); and, besides these, even impersonal things, such as apostasy, godlessness, the Catholic Church, and, to mention only one other thing, Smallpox. In a revelation of Jesus Christ men would fain expect to read nothing less than every thing which had determined the fate of humanity since its appearance. In proportion as people could show for certain that what had already happened was prophesied in it, they might also rest assured that all that it said about a time still to come would be correctly unravelled.

All this mass of ingenuity and error might of course have been seen from the beginning to be useless, if people had only taken note, amongst other things, of the first verse and the last verse but one in the book. We are told in i. 1 (and xxii. 6) that the revelation of Jesus Christ is "to shew unto his servants the things which must shortly come to pass." And this does not mean "which must soon begin, and then go on for thousands of years," for in xxii. 20 (as well as in iii. 11; xxii. 7, 12) Jesus says, "I come quickly," that is to say, to introduce the end of the world. The author of the book, accordingly, expected the end of the world in his own lifetime; and if we wish to understand the curious figures in which he described it, we must try to interpret them in the light of the ideas which prevailed at the time.

2. COMBINATION OF SEPARATE FRAGMENTS.

But first we must realise clearly that in this book we have not to do with a single author. The visions which he is supposed to have seen in it follow upon one another with so little regard to order that it has already been thought that he could not have seen them all one after another, but after each must have had time to note it down; other wise he would not have been in a position to note them all in their right order. No less than six times we find the "last things," which from what has already been said we might think are to follow (viii. 1; xi. 15-19; xiv. 20; xvi. 17-21; xviii. 21-24; xix. 21), described before the real conclusion of the book. In every case we meet with a self-contained picture only in a particular section of the narrative, and for the most part this never extends to a whole chapter.

It has been noticed that chap. xxiv. of Mt.'s Gospel (not so literally in Mk. xiii., and in Lk. xxi. in a version which differs still more) incorporates a very small publication in which events are described which are supposed to happen immediately before or at the end of the world. Mt. xxiv. 6-8, 15-22, 29-31, 34, that is to say, do not fit into the sections between which they are placed, but connect together all the better. These verses, which have been called a "little Apocalypse," and which now appear as the words of Jesus only by an entire misapprehension, may very well have been a leaflet published and spread abroad at the time of direst need in order to call the attention of the faithful to signs by which they might recognise the near approach of the end of the world, and to warn them. In xxiv. 15 we even read, "let him that readeth under stand," though Jesus would have been obliged to say, "let him that heareth."

Such leaflets may still be discovered in the Apocalypse of Jn. as well. It is difficult to say whether the writer who put together the whole book was the first to insert them, or whether earlier workers did so, each of them publishing only a part of the present book; and the matter is of subordinate importance. Particular stones in the building attract attention and can be separated more easily than those sections of the walls which have been constructed by one or another foreman.

3. A LEAFLET ON THE FATE OF JERUSALEM.

In Rev. xi. 1-13 we can recognise a leaflet which is quite similar to the little Apocalypse in Mt. xxiv., and belongs to the last years before August 70 A.D., when the Temple at Jerusalem was destroyed by the Imperial Prince, Titus. We learn from xi. 1 f. that the heathen might tread upon the outer fore-court of the Temple and the rest of the holy city of Jerusalem, but might not touch "the temple of God, and the altar, and them that worship therein." Often enough two, and even three, hostile parties had struggled for months without result inside the walls of Jerusalem. Just before Easter of the year 70 one of the three parties was in possession of the Temple with the inner fore-court, the other of the rest of the Temple hill, the third of the rest of the city. The author was therefore entirely justified by the events of the time in his expectation, even if in the end he was baffled by the destruction of the Temple.

He cannot, of course, have been a Christian if Jesus supposed prophecy, "there shall not be left here one stone upon another" (Mk. xiii. 2), was well known. And Jesus may very well have uttered such a prophecy, even if we refuse to credit him with omniscience. By simply exercising human powers of reflection, it was not difficult to foresee the fall of the Temple. But since this prophecy may also have been ascribed to Jesus subsequently, it is still possible that it was a Christian who gave expression to the contrary prophecy in his leaflet (Rev. xi. 1-13).

4. PROPHECY CONCERNING ROME AND THE FIRST BEAST.

But the city of Rome takes an even more important place than Jerusalem in the Apocalypse. Fear of the authorities, who might think the prophecies about it dangerous to the State, leads the author to mention the city not by its real name, but by that of Babylon, which, as was well known, was in the Old Testament associated with an equal amount of wickedness; but xvii. 5 f., 9, 18 make it clear enough to every intelligent reader what city is meant. In chap. xviii., which, like xi. 1-13, may have been a separate leaflet, the description of its overthrow is quite different from that given in the other parts of the book.

In these we find connected with it the most important figure in the whole Apocalypse, the (first) beast, that is to say, the Roman imperium. It supports and carries the woman, as the city of Rome is also called (xvii. 3, 7), it has a throne, kingdom, dominion over the world (xiii. 2, 7; xvi. 10), and, in particular, seven heads, that is to say, as we learn in xvii. 9 f., seven kings, of whom the first five have fallen, one is now reigning, and the seventh is still to come. The first five Roman emperors, who are here intended, were Augustus, Tiberius, Caligula, Claudius, and Nero. The author of chap. xvii. therefore writes after Nero's death, which took place on the 9th of June in the year 68; and the same date suits chap. xiii. Nero, it is true, had no real successors; but Galba, Otho, and Vitellius struggled for the mastery until Vespasian seized it for himself in December of the year 69. Yet it is by no means certain that he was numbered as the sixth, and that the one and a half years of the dispute about the succession are excluded. A person who lived in the second half of the year 68 could only say, as our author does, "the sixth emperor is now reigning," though in other parts of the extensive Roman empire his rule was disputed.

There is something else which suggests that the time intended is that immediately following Nero's death. By the beast we are not always meant to understand the Roman imperium in general, but sometimes a single emperor. There is no mistake when it is said in xiii. 7 f., "and there was given to him (that is to say, the beast) authority over every tribe . . . and all that dwell on the earth shall worship him" and in xiii. 14, "to the beast who hath the stroke of the sword, and lived." Add to this xvii. 8, 11: "the beast . . . was and (now) is not, and is about to come up out of the abyss . . . and the beast that was, and is not, is himself the eighth, and at the same time is one of the seven (Roman Emperors), and he goeth into perdition."

To which Roman Emperor does this apply? When Nero saw that his rule was at an end, he fled in the company of a few persons to an estate, and on hearing his pursuers approaching, with the help of his secretary he cut his throat with a sword. His corpse was solemnly burned. But his friends, especially amongst the mob, refused to believe that he was dead; they imagined that he had made his escape and would shortly return and wrest back his power.

A heathen could not reconcile these two accounts of Nero's end; but a Christian (or a Jew), believing as he did in a resurrection, could very well do so. Accordingly, all that we read about the beast in the Apocalypse would apply to Nero: the sword-wound, the death, the return from the underworld, to which every one went when he died, and the statement that this risen person who is to appear as the eighth emperor, was one of the seven preceding emperors. We know indeed that impostors were continually coming forward and claiming to be Nero. The very first, who arose as early as the year in which Nero died, created a disturbance for months along the whole of the west coast of Asia Minor as well as in Greece. And this makes it probable that these sections of the Apocalypse date from that time, and so from 68 or 69.

Those who, as we mentioned above, claim that the sixth place must be assigned to the Emperor Vespasian, and that this was the reign in which the author lived, may still discover the reason for his statements in the appearance of this false Nero, if they suppose that they were written in the first period of Vespasian, that is to say at the be ginning of the year 70. On the other hand, the next false Nero of whom we hear did not appear at the end of the reign of Vespasian, but in the days of his successor, Titus. But a person who wrote in this reign (79-81) could in no circumstances say that he was living in the reign of the sixth Emperor.

It has been thought that the expectation that the resuscitated Nero would be the eighth Emperor could only have been held when the seventh had already ascended the throne; otherwise a seventh would not have been prophesied. But the writer's conviction that Rome would have seven emperors was drawn from the Old Testament book of Daniel. This represents the matter in such a way that it might have been composed in the sixth century B.C. (in reality it was not written until 167-164 B.C.), and prophesies in vii. 1-8 that there will appear one after another a lion, a bear, a panther with four heads, and another terrible beast with ten horns. According to vii. 17, what are meant are four empires which will rule the world one after another, the Babylonian down to 539 B.C., the Median which really ended as early as 550, the Persian, 539-330, to which the author assigns four kings instead of eleven, and the Greek with ten kings in Syria, to the last among whom the Jews were subject.

Since the author of the Apocalypse does not pretend, like the book of Daniel, to prophesy so many centuries before the time in which he really lived, he speaks of only one world-wide empire, that of Home. Since, however, the book of Daniel and its description of the empires ruling the world was held to be a divine prophecy, which in the author's lifetime still waited for fulfilment, he (or one of his predecessors) has made its four beasts into one, which now, according to xiii. 1 f., has at the same time the characteristics of the lion, the bear, and the panther, and the ten horns of the fourth beast, but the seven heads of all four which these have all together. The idea that the end of the world is at hand is reckoned with, in spite of the seventh emperor, by representing in xvii. 10 that he will reign for a short time.

Here again we can note well how the Apocalypse borrows its descriptions from an older prophecy, which it held to be sacred, and how at the same time it adapts this prophecy to its own present. This enables us to understand fully such a figure as that of the beast, which is really very curious. In other cases as well, the author continually takes his expressions and even whole sentences from the Old Testament. It may be, however, that several remarkable descriptions in the book are derived from other old prophecies, perhaps suggested by myths about the gods of the Babylonians or Persians.

5. THE NUMBER 666.

The last point which confirms us in thinking that Nero is meant by the beast consists in the famous number (xiii. 18): "He that hath understanding, let him count the number of the beast; for it is the number of a man; and his number is six hundred and sixty and six." The number of a man, or as it is said in xiii. 17, the number of the name of the beast is the number which results when all the numbers are added which are indicated by the letters of the name. In Latin only a few letters (I, V, X, L, C, M, D) are used for numbers, but in Greek and Hebrew all. Now the number 666 does really result when we write N(e)ron K(e)s(a)r (that is to say, Emperor Nero) in Hebrew letters and add up the numbers: 50 + 200 + 6 + 50 + 100 + 60 + 200 (the letters in brackets are not written in Hebrew). The number 666 also results from more than a hundred other solutions which have been suggested. But, apart from other reasons which show that the many popes, princes, and so forth down to the present time which people have tried to find in the beast, cannot be intended, no such calculation has been hit upon which might at the same time give 616 as the correct number. And yet there must be this alternative, for in many copies of the Apocalpyse even before the time of Irenaeus, that is to say, before 185, 616 is given as the number instead of 666, And this is the number we get if an "n" is omitted from Neron Kesar, which represents the number 50: Nero Kesar. This, too, would suit very well, for where Latin was spoken people said Nero, whereas the Greek form, familiar to the author of the Apocalypse himself, is Neron. It was natural to him to use Hebrew for the calculation, for in any case it was his mother-tongue, and it would make it less easy for uninitiated persons to solve the riddle. Irenaeus himself no longer knew the solution. It was rejected because Nero failed to return.

6. TIME OF COMPOSITION.

The most important sections of the book, that concerning Jerusalem, and those about the return of Nero from the underworld, date therefore in all probability from the years 68-70. None of the others indicates so clearly the date at which it came into existence. We ask therefore at once when the whole book may be supposed to have been put together. And here Irenaeus tells us that the Apocalypse was revealed and written down at the end of the reign of the Emperor Domitian, that is to say, in the year 95 or 96. We have already seen (p. 194 f.) how little we can rely on Irenaeus in such matters. But in this case we have no definite reason to dispute that the date he fixes for the composition of the Apocalypse is appropriate enough for the putting together of the whole book.

7. THE AUTHOR NOT THE AUTHOR OF THE FOURTH GOSPEL.

But who is the author (or compiler) of the whole Apocalypse? In any case, it is not the same person who wrote the Fourth Gospel. The two works are fundamentally different.

If the Gospel is not written in good Greek style, the style is at any rate smooth; the Apocalypse has very serious linguistic mistakes. Moreover, in both works Jesus is called the Lamb, but in each case a different Greek word is used. The Evangelist knows nothing about the things which are most important to the author of the Apocalypse, about the terrible events before the end of the world, about the descent of Christ and his army from the sky on white horses for the great battle with the kings of the earth, about the peaceful millennial rule of the faithful after their resurrection, about the Jerusalem which is to come down from heaven and is 12,000 stadia--say, a third of the radius of the earth--in length, breadth, and height, and consists of gold transparent like glass (xix. 11-21; xx. 1-6; xxi. 9-xxii. 5), &c.; and he cannot have wished to know anything about these things, since his style of thought was averse to all such expectations. Nor may we go so far as to assume that both men belonged to one and the same circle of kindred spirits. The most we can say is that the Apocalypse may have still been held in honour by those who held the same views as the Evangelist; he himself was far superior to its style of thought, and shows only in isolated cases that he was familiar with it but not, for in stance, where it is said that Jesus "is the Logos of God." In Rev. xix. 13 this is a later addition, for his name "no one knoweth, but he himself" (verse 12).

8. THE AUTHOR NOT THE APOSTLE JOHN.

As we cannot ascribe the Gospel to the Apostle John, it is still possible that he may have written the Apocalypse (in i. 1, 4 the author calls himself John and a servant of Christ; in xxii. 9 a prophet). But, in that case we may be sure he would not call Jesus, exactly as if he were God, the Alpha and Omega, that is to say, as is expressly explained, the first and the last (literally the first and last letter of the Greek Alphabet; see xxii. 13; i. 17; ii. 8, just as in i. 8; xxi. 6), nor describe him as the first link of God's creation, if not as the author of God's creation (iii. 14). We found such expressions in the Fourth Gospel, but not in the Synoptics. And how can a personal disciple of Jesus imagine him in heaven as a lamb with seven horns and seven eyes, "standing as though it had been slain," and then taking a book from the hand of God and breaking its seals (v. 6-9; vi. 1), or conceive of him as he is described in i. 13-16? But even if he took such sections as these from another book and incorporated them in his own, we might expect that expression would be given at the same time to his own recollection of the life of Jesus. And yet almost the only case in which this is done is in the statement that Jesus is "the true witness" (i. 5; iii. 14), and we cannot be sure that this does not mean that Jesus is now testifying in heaven that what is prophesied in the Apocalypse is true (such is the idea in i. 2). We need only add that according to xxi. 14 the names of the twelve Apostles of the Lamb, that is to say, of Christ, are written on the twelve foundation-stones of the walls of the heavenly Jerusalem. Had one of these same apostles written this or even merely incorporated it in his book, we should be obliged to regard it in the same way as the title, "the disciple whom Jesus loved," if by this the Fourth Evangelist meant himself (pp. 179-181).

9. THE AUTHOR JOHN THE ELDER?

It is different if we think of John the Elder (p. 172 f.) as the final editor of the Apocalypse. This would explain the fact (which would also be appropriate if the author were the Apostle John) that the Jews are always represented as the chosen people of God (vii. 1-8), and that it is forbidden to eat flesh taken from a victim offered to a heathen idol (ii. 14, 20), though Paul declared it to have been allowed in principle (1 Cor. x. 25-27, 29b, 30) and only forbids it when a sensitive Christian who thought it for bidden might be offended by it (1 Cor. viii. 7-13; x. 28, 29 a), or when people, by sharing in the festivities, recognised the idol as a real god (1 Cor. x. 20 f .) In this matter a strongly Jewish sentiment in favour of the Law of the Old Testament still pervades the Apocalypse.

We know further, as regards John the Elder (but not also as regards the Apostle), that he was very much interested in prophecies of the end of the world, and imagined, for example, that after the resurrection of the dead there would be on earth a millennial kingdom full of peace and happiness and ruled by Christ, exactly as it is described in Rev. xx. 1-6.

When we remember, finally, that John the Elder of Ephesus was leader of the Church of Western Asia Minor, we can easily see how well his position suits the tone in which the seven Epistles to the seven Communities in that region are composed in Rev. ii. f. They were certainly not sent separately to each one of those communities, and grouped together only at a later date. The way in which they are all written round the same circle of ideas, and almost modelled on one pattern, indicates far rather that from the very first they were only intended for publication in the book of Revelation. They make a weighty impression precisely because the same turns of expression recur so continually. They must, therefore, in any case, have been composed by the last contributor to the book, with the idea of recommending a definite circle of readers to take due note of the prophecies which follow in iv. 1-xxii. 5.

Jews, all those points are touched upon which were in question between Christians and Jews in the second century: Jesus is really the Son of God; the Jews refusal to believe this is simply due to obstinacy, &c. In this way, the author answers all the needs of his time. We must leave the question whether there were also followers of John the Baptist to be refuted, and whether it is against these that proof is offered of the great superiority of Jesus (p. 80).

3. APPRECIATION OF MONTANISM AND GNOSTICISM.

We see more clearly how the author appreciates those intellectual movements of his age with which he feels that he him self has something in common. He prepared the way even for Montanus of Phrygia and his followers, who after the year 156 came forward with new prophecies and declared that this age of theirs, the age of the Holy Spirit which filled them, represented a higher level compared with the time in which Jesus lived, by making Jesus himself say in Jn. xvi. 12 f., that the disciples could not at the time understand many other things which he had to say to them, but that after his death the Holy Spirit would come and lead them into all truth.

But it was, in particular, the captivating ideas of Gnosticism that the Fourth Evangelist appropriated (pp. 152 f. 158-160). He did a great service to his age by showing that one could be a thinker, appreciate knowledge, stand in the midst of a stream of thoroughly intellectual movements, and yet remain a faithful son of the Church. In this way, we may presume, he contributed not a little to keep Christians from splitting into two classes having hardly any connecting link, the intellectual aristocracy of the Gnostics and simple believers. In face of mutual feuds and of persecution from without, such cleavage might have endangered the continued existence of Christianity altogether. The Second and Third Epistles of John, which aimed at keeping the communities closely knit together by means of the authority of the Church, also deserve part of the credit for having warded off this danger. To us the effort may not seem, very exalted or even very beautiful: but, nevertheless, it was productive of good.

4. IDEAS ABOUT THE STATE AFTER DEATH.

The Fourth Evangelist, by adopting the view that the visible world is only a perishable copy of the invisible, at the same time introduced a revolution in the ideas about the state after death, the results of which have been felt even down to the present time. The Old Testament, and with it Jesus and the whole of primitive Christendom, imagined a future state of happiness upon earth. Even in the Apocalypse (xxi. 1 f.), we read of the New Jerusalem descending from heaven upon a renovated earth.

Only in a few passages does Paul express the idea (2 Cor. v. 1-8; Phil. i. 23) that the faithful immediately after their death will come to Christ in heaven. It is not until we turn to the Epistle to the Hebrews (xii. 27 f.) that we find the teaching that at the end of things the earth will pass away entirely and only the heavens remain; there, in the heavenly Jerusalem, which will not descend upon earth, is also the place where Christians will enjoy eternal happiness (xii. 22 f.). But whereas this truth is not easily to be discovered in the Epistle to the Hebrews, in Jn. it is expressed with absolute clearness (xiv. 2): "in my Father's house are many mansions. . . I go," by being exalted to heaven, "to prepare a place for you."

5. JESUS THE SON OF GOD AND LOGOS IN HEAVEN.

But the Fourth Evangelist exercised the greatest influence by adopting to some extent the view of the world held by the great thinkers of his age and applying it to the Person of Jesus. Paul and those who followed him (pp. 144-146) had already ascribed to Jesus a life with God in heaven before his descent upon earth, and even a share in the creation of the world; but Jn. is the first to start clearly with the idea that Jesus was the Logos and that without him God could have produced no effect upon the world, because He, being perfectly good, was obliged without question to keep at a distance from the world which was thoroughly evil. The idea that Jesus was begotten of God as a human son is begotten by his human father, an idea which Paul and those who followed him had given expression to before Jn., must of itself have helped very much to make Gentiles familiar with Jesus from the start and favourably disposed towards his worship, for they knew of and worshipped so many deities who were begotten by a god. But the statement was truly a greater one when it could be said that the Logos, whose work the deepest thinkers had found to be necessary if the divine influence was to come into the world, was no other than Jesus. While the conception of Jesus as a Son of God might make an impression on the lower classes among the Gentiles, that of Jesus as the Logos would attract the people of culture. And, as a matter of fact, it was very important that Christianity should not always remain a religion merely for uncultured and uninfluential people. In the form in which the Fourth Gospel presented it, it was capable of satisfying the highest demands of the age. Here attention was no longer paid to the fact that this Jesus in whom people were to believe was a Jew--a fact which might have greatly repelled many Gentiles--for he is described in such a way as to make him quite superior to everything Jewish. And so Jn., even more than Paul, has brought it about that Jesus should be recognised as being what he was--without Jesus himself thinking the idea out--the Saviour of the world.

6. EMPHASIS ON THE CHURCH.

True, there is another side to this picture. There was now no longer any other way of attaining to blessedness than by believing in Jesus. He himself must now be represented as continually requiring people to believe in him--a request which the Jesus of the Synoptics made so seldom. The branches must abide in the vine (by which Jesus means himself), otherwise they will wither. "Apart from me ye can do nothing" (xv. 4 f.). But this means at the same time that one must be a member of the Church and submit to the ordinances of the Church; for example, to those of the Second Epistle of John (verse 10 f.), which forbids one to receive Christian brethren who hold different doctrines, or even to greet them. People are now divided into those who are in communion with the Church and are blessed, and those who are outside and are not; and the fact that one belongs to the Church is apt, moreover, to depend more on faith than on that doing of the will of God which Jesus required so continually in the Synoptics. On the other hand, the feeling that one is one of the elect leads only too readily to presumption; the power which is associated with ecclesiastical officialism leads to domination, and even, in certain circumstances, to mercenariness (1 Pet. v. 2; 1 Tim. iii. 8).

Nevertheless, it was necessary to establish a Church communion. The desire to enjoy a common religious possession with people of a like mind cannot be repressed. Moreover, such communion is a powerful support to the individual, whether he comes to be distressed by doubts, is in trouble, or is in danger of falling into sin. Institutions which serve this purpose, whatever dangers may lurk in them, must be considered instruments of progress.

To all intents and purposes, the Fourth Evangelist never speaks of such institutions (xxi. 15-17 is by a later writer; see p. 186 f.). He has no interest whatever in episcopal authority and such like things. Had he had, it would have been a simple matter to make Jesus say something more than he does in xx. 21-23 about the privileges of the Apostles. His idea of the Church is still thoroughly ideal a community with Christ alone as its head. Nevertheless, we should make a great mistake if we were to think that he is indifferent to the Church. Every one who wishes to be blessed must share the Church's belief in Jesus; he who does not share it is already judged (iii. 18). He who wishes to be a shepherd of the Church must come in to the sheep through the door, which is Jesus himself, that is to say, through faith in him (x. 7-9; see p. 135). Indeed, according to the one point of view, with which, it is true, we shall soon have to contrast another, no man can have life in him unless he partakes of the Supper (vi. 51b-56).

But beyond question the author, while emphasising these thoughts, does so in moderation. In the First Epistle of John, the believer's consciousness that he comes from God, possesses full knowledge, and is free from sin (iv. 4, 6; ii. 20 f., 27; iii. 9; v. 18 by the side of i. 8-ii. 2: "if any man sin, we have an advocate with the Father, Jesus), certainly goes very far; but it is due to a connection with Gnosticism, more than to the idea that one belongs to the Church. Both authors never forget that it is the individual who must have the faith and keep the commandments of God; they do not say that, because he is a member of the Church, any demand which should really be required of him will be lessened. If, on the one hand, the Church is a blessing, and so far as it is an evil, on the other hand, is a necessary evil, we shall have to admit that only the Second and Third Epistles of Jn. transgress the limits of what has to be recognised as an appropriate move forward.

7. JESUS AS A DIVINE BEING UPON EARTH.

The really dangerous aspect of the matter when, by describing Jesus as the Son of God and the Logos, people easily induced the Gentiles to believe in him, is seen in another direction. They had to carry this description through. It had to be shown in detail how be walked on earth as a divine being, simply proclaiming his high rank, doing the greatest miracles for his own glorification, and for that reason keeping away from the grave of Lazarus for two days, while at the same time an effort had to be made to maintain that he was really a man. We need not stop again to explain how difficult it is for the mind to imagine this figure, or how hard it is for the religious sentiment to accept it. Even if it were applied to the Jesus of the Synoptics, that would be a hard saying: "I am the way and the truth and the life; no man cometh unto the Father but by me" (xiv. 6). People without number have either never had an opportunity of hearing about him, or in spite of knowing of him, hold to another religion or to a way of thinking which cannot ascribe any merits to some mediator who has appeared at some previous date; and yet, as a matter of fact, they display as much humility, love, and fidelity to God as the many Christians who have devoted themselves to the faith of the Church. But how much harder is the saying, when it is the Jesus of the Fourth Gospel in whom one must believe unconditionally if one wishes to enter into communion with God!

For centuries this demand has been made and complied with; and the books of history suggest rarely to some extent how many have been the doubts, and how great has been the torture of souls. To-day, in ever widening circles, people resolutely refuse to comply with it. And since this has happened, it may be considered fortunate that Jn. has made the demand so emphatically. For as a result of it we have been made to decide that no further move can be made in his direction, and that we must go back to the Synoptics and try to find in their account and--with their own guidance--in the background of their account, the figure of Jesus as he really existed.

8. WHY DID JN. WRITE A GOSPEL?

But why did this person write a Gospel? We are sure that the question has long ago occurred to many of our readers. But what other kind of book should he have written? A treatise, or a letter like the First Epistle of Jn. as found in our Bible? What does this contain? Hardly anything but general maxims: we must love God, we must shun false teachers. Now the Gospel also contains such maxims: God is Spirit; a man must be born from above (iv. 24, iii. 3), and so forth. But Christianity does not purpose to be a system of Wisdom, based upon theory; it is a religion which appeals to Jesus. Therefore in a book which is to make an impression he must be represented as coming forward and saying: "a new commandment I give unto you, that ye love one another;" "I am the Light of the world;" "I am the Bread of Life;" "I am the Resurrection and the Life" (xiii. 34; viii. 12; vi. 35; xi. 25). At Jesus hand the Christians, and with them the Fourth Evangelist, wished to receive no less than all that they thought themselves entitled to hope for. And, similarly, if all the blessings which still make Christianity precious to us at the present day were to be brought into the world of the Gentiles, it was of all things necessary that Jesus should be recognised by them; it was necessary therefore to record his acts, especially if the Gnostics introduced the danger of resolving his earthly life into a mere phantom existence (p. 150).

And it was necessary to be able to describe everything as being as sublime as possible. It would not do to stop short at the teaching of Paul, that Jesus laid aside his divine attributes before he came down from heaven. If he ever possessed them, he must actually reveal them, and reveal them just where they could be seen by human eyes--upon earth. This idea must necessarily have arisen sooner or later. The higher the god, the more powerful his help; and Gentiles, who hitherto had always turned from a god who was not sufficiently powerful to one who was supposed to be more so, would only address themselves to a powerful god. In fact, even if Jn. had refrained from writing a Gospel, another person would have written one in the same sense, and we should simply have to make our complaint elsewhere.

9. SOME SPECIAL IDEAS OF ABIDING VALUE.

What we have said may have suggested that the Fourth Gospel with the Epistles of Jn. met the needs of its age in a very successful way, but hardly gives us anything that is of value for all times. Certainly, the abiding worth of the Gospel is not to be found where people seek it, and where the claim of the book itself, that it is a history of the life and work of Jesus, implies that they must seek it. Nevertheless, it is seen to be all the greater in other respects.

If the authors of the Gospel and the First Epistle were not thinkers in the strict sense of the term, but have taken up philosophical ideas simply in order to defend their own religion, yet by their declarations, "God is Spirit" (Jn. iv. 24: that is to say, God is of spiritual nature; not, God is a spirit) and "God is Love" (1 Jn. iv. 8, 16), they have expressed the nature of God with a precision which cannot be surpassed. Their leaning towards Gnosticism has given them other ideas of abiding value: a deep-rooted feeling of dependence upon God (Jn. iii. 27; pp. 149 f., 159 f.), and that interest in knowledge and truth which no religion can ever dispense with. And yet, at the same time, the onesidedness to which this might lead is obviated by the fact that what is made the test of knowing God is the keeping of his commandments (1 Jn. ii. 3).

Equally deep is the truth hidden in the saying of Jesus (Jn. vii. 17): "If any man willeth to do his will, he shall know of the teaching, whether it be of God, or whether I speak from myself." The context shows that by the will of God, which is to be kept, is meant, not the command to live a moral life, but nothing else than that teaching of Jesus which consists in declaring that people must believe in his divine origin. They will find this to be true as soon as they humbly accept it. Whether this statement is correct is another question. But it carries us farther than its application in this passage. It contains a criterion which is true in all cases and will show how man, to whom the knowledge whether a thing is of God has been made so difficult, can learn in another way, by trial, by a provisional submission of his will, whether it will satisfy him to such an extent that he can rest assured that it is divine.

10. COMMUNION WITH GOD.

The First Epistle of John speaks in most beautiful language of what is at the heart of religion, communion with God. In the Gospel, since it is assumed that God is separated from the world, this communion is always effected through Jesus, who says, for example, in xvii. 23, "I in them, and thou in me"; according to the Epistle, man himself, without a mediator, feels that God is in him and that he is in God (p. 209 f.). This mysticism, the intenseness of which remains, whether it consist in a feeling of union with God, or with Christ, is something peculiar to the Johannine Writings. Nowhere else in the New Testament has it so profound a meaning; in most cases, indeed, the gap between man and God, and man and Christ, is represented as being so great that the writers cannot imagine any such union. In the Johannine Writings the idea at the same time serves in a valuable way to counter balance the emphasis laid on knowledge, and thus assigns the feelings the place that rightfully belongs to them in religion.

The actualisation of this close communion with God, however, is found in love of God to man and of man to God, and from these in turn flows the love of the brethren for one another. Not even Paul in the thirteenth chapter of the First Epistle to the Corinthians has written anything more profound about love than that found in the First Epistle of John (iii. 13-18; iv. 7-21). The original source of love, it tells us, is God. Our love for Him and for the brethren only flow from His love; but it should do so for the very reason that God first loved us. It is of the very essence of love for God that we should keep those commandments of His which are not hard when they are obeyed from love, and that all fear of Him should vanish. In fact, though God is originally unknown, through our love to the brethren, he becomes perceptible as one who is present in our souls. And the Fourth Evangelist could not have summarised the life-work of Jesus more appropriately than he does when he makes him say (xiii. 34 f .): "A new commandment I give unto you, that ye love one another. . . . By this shall all men know that ye are my disciples, if ye have love one to another." In this way, as a matter of fact, he turns from his great doctrines about Jesus dignity and his derivation from God, to the simplest fact which the Synoptics tell us about him.

11. REDEMPTION THROUGH JESUS.

He does this again, though with a different result, in what he says about the redemption brought by Jesus. According to the Synoptics, Jesus emancipated (redeemed) those who attached themselves to him from two kinds of illusion and from two kinds of sin: from the illusions of a religion of fear, and of a religion of pretences, as it is represented in the parable in Lk. (xviii. 9-14) by the Pharisee as distinguished from the publican, and from the sins of selfishness and worldliness (Mt. xvi. 25 f.). He does so by proclaiming his teaching, by illustrating it by his own example, and by his death, which proves that he is ready not merely to come forward and champion his cause, but even to die for it. Remission of guilt, forgiveness of sins, was included in this emancipation from the religion of fear. He is not in the least aware that his death is required in order that God may be merciful out of consideration for the sacrifice. When he promises the spiritually poor, the meek, the merciful, those who do God's will, and those who become like children, that they shall enjoy the Kingdom of Heaven, no previous conditions are laid down (Mt. v. 3-9; vii. 21; xviii. 3); when in the parable in Lk. (xv. 11-32) the lost son returns home penitent, his father goes to meet him, falls on his neck and kisses him without asking whether any one has offered a sacrifice for him; while Jesus is still present amongst his followers, he teaches them to pray "Forgive us our sins," and comforts them with the words, "Come unto me, all ye that are weary and heavy-laden, and I will refresh you" (Mt. vi. 12; xi. 28). Picture to yourself a scene in which some poor child of man, burdened with guilt, casts himself at Jesus' feet and asks that he may realise this promise. Had Jesus thought his own death necessary before forgiveness of sin could be realised, he would have been obliged to say to him: "No, no, I did not mean that; you must wait until I have died for you on the cross." And yet before the declaration in Mt. xi. 28 he was silent about it!

On the last evening of his life, Jesus said: "this is my body;" "this is my blood of the covenant, which is shed for many" (Mk. xiv. 22-24). But only Mt. tells us that he added "for forgiveness of sins;" and in the words, which have been thought so sacred, and moreover from the first have been repeated at every celebration of the Supper, we may be certain, nothing was omitted. On the other hand, additions might certainly be made; the person who officiated at the celebration would first express something as his own idea, and then at a later date this would be wrongly regarded as a saying of Jesus (we have a very clear example in the introductory words, "take," "eat," in Mt., of which Mk. has only one, and Paul, in 1 Cor. xi. 24, and Lk. neither).

In what sense Jesus thought of shedding his blood for many, we can easily realise when we remember that he was reclining at the paschal meal (pp. 117-130). God had promised to pass by those houses, the doors of which were smeared with the blood of the Paschal lamb, when on the night before the Exodus of the Israelites with Moses from Egypt, he would kill all the first-born (Exod. xii. 7, 12 f.; 21-27). The lamb, therefore, had to die that others might be spared from death. In like manner, Jesus will give his life to the fury of the enemy, that his followers, whose lives would otherwise have been equally threatened, might escape, since after their Master's death people would think them harmless. We see then that he certainly wished to make his death a sacrifice, not, however, in order that they might have forgiveness of sins, but that they might be preserved from misfortune, and from a misfortune which they did not deserve. [8] And if he added further, that his blood was the blood of a covenant, his idea was that he was again knitting them closely to God by a covenant, and that in the Old Testament whenever such a covenant was made a sacrificial victim was slain (Jer. xxxiv. 18; Gen. xv. 10, 17 f.; Exod. xxiv. 3-8). Here again there is no idea of a sacrifice for sin.

And the only other passage in the Synoptics in which Jesus attaches importance to his death for the salvation of men, can be understood in the same way as the paschal sacrifice: "for verily the Son of Man came not to be ministered unto, but to minister, and to give his life a ransom for many" (Mk. x. 45 = Mt. xx. 28), that is to say, that they might be spared from the danger of themselves falling victims to persecution. Instead of the Greek word "ransom," Jesus, who spoke Aramaic, may very well have used a word which simply meant "an instrument of escape." If, however, a sacrifice for the forgiveness of sins were really intended, we should be compelled to suspect that the concluding words ("and to give his life" . . .) are a later addition based upon an idea of the Apostle Paul, since they would be in contradiction with all that we have just found in the Synoptics. As far as the context is concerned, they can be dispensed with at once, and are not found in Lk. (xxii. 27) where the introductory words (in a somewhat different version) occur.

Paul or some of his predecessors (1 Cor. xv. 3), with their strictly Jewish way of thinking, introduced into Christianity the idea that God was so angry with men for their sins that he had decreed the eternal destruction of all of them, and could only have mercy upon them if his own son died on the cross as a sacrifice on their behalf. In doing so, according to the opinion of Paul, Jesus took upon him the punishment of death which originally men themselves deserved; but he took it upon him as one who was guilt less, and therefore his offering became a sin-offering to God. This view has been held fast to in Church doctrine down to the present day, regardless of the fact that it is not found at all in the Synoptics, and only sporadically in the Fourth Gospel (p. 209), and that in the New Testament the purpose of Jesus' death is described in more than twenty different ways, [9] which would not certainly have been the case if people had known of one generally satis factory explanation.

If, as the Fourth Gospel represents, Jesus is the Logos, it cannot have been through his death that he first brought redemption. He is supposed to bring the world into conformity with God's will, since God himself was obliged to avoid contact with it. This he could only do by his own activity, and so, when upon earth, by his works and preaching. According to Jn., he may be compared especially with the light which shines upon the world; and so the only important question is whether people turn to him or away from him (iii. 19-21; i. 4-13). If they do the former (that is to say, as Jn. puts it, believe in him), they are quit of sin from that hour. But this brings us at once face to face with a character which is familiar to us from the Synoptics. In the Synoptics also Jesus brings salvation by his words and works, not by his death; and declares that people's sins are forgiven at once, wherever he finds the right frame of mind (Mk. ii. 5, 9; Lk. vii. 47 f.).

May we suppose then that Jn. here preserves a correct recollection of the Life of Jesus? Certainly not. He only arrives at this agreement with the Synoptics after making an extraordinarily roundabout journey. Paul, influenced by a kind of piety which was very conscientious, and for that reason very punctilious, in his teaching about the sacrificial death of Jesus introduced foreign matter into the Gospel. Jn., though in a tacit and quiet way, removes it again. Had he remembered that it was not originally part of the Gospel, he would have omitted it altogether, whereas, as a matter of fact, he uses it several times (i. 29, 36; on xi. 50-52; xvii. 19b, see pp. 271, 272 f.). It is not used by him in other places, simply because it could not easily be adapted to the other new matter which he felt obliged of his own accord to introduce into the Gospel of Jesus, we mean to the doctrine that Jesus was the Logos. To this doctrine itself he had only been led by that other mistake made by Paul when he supposed that Jesus was begotten as the Son of God before the creation of the world, and had existed in heaven down to the time of his descent upon earth. The idea that he was the Logos only carries us one step beyond this teaching. And yet it is this alone that gives rise to the doctrine that Jesus brought redemption, not by his death, but by his appearance upon earth. Thus we have here an exemplification of the great law of intellectual progress, that very often one truth proceeds from another only by the pathway of error. Jn. only succeeded in arriving at the truth which already existed in the Life of Jesus, by adopting the second of Paul's mistakes and carrying it farther.

We ourselves, nevertheless, have reason to rejoice at the result. We no longer find in Jn. any of Paul's laborious arguments to prove that the Jewish Law has ceased to be binding upon Christians, and that the sinner is justified, that is to say, is declared righteous by God, through faith. If God is to declare any one righteous, he must be represented as a judge, and must as such examine one's works; and the faith which the sinner has merely to exhibit will not be a work, but the opposite of any kind of service: it must be simply trust, purely the opening of the hand to receive a gift from God--and this, moreover, is what it really is. Paul himself in truth found it very difficult to preserve intact the most deeply-rooted feature of this kind of faith, for with him faith always involved the acceptance as unimpeachable true of two facts of the past which criticism might only too easily shatter, and as a matter of fact has shattered altogether. The first is that Jesus suffered death for the purpose of blotting out the sins of mankind; the second that he rose from the dead after three days.

Now, the latter Jn. also requires us to believe, that is to say, to accept as true; but the faith in Jesus person which Jn. asks for--although it also includes acceptance of the truth of his heavenly origin--consists again, exactly as it does in the Synoptics, simply in feeling oneself drawn to him, in confiding in him, in recognising him as one's redeemer. Similarly--in place of the above-noted difficulties in Paul's teaching about justification by faith--in the Johannine writings everything has once more become so simple that the important matter is again, just as in the Synoptics, to do the will of God or Jesus, concerning which especially the First Epistle of John speaks in such beautiful language (ii. 3 f., iii. 22, 24, v. 3 f.; Jn. viii. 51, xiv. 21, xv. 10, 14). In fact, when Jesus washes his disciples' feet he speaks of it simply as an example which he is giving them (xiii. 14 f.), an idea, for a parallel to which we shall search in vain in many writings of the New Testament. If the roundabout way by which the author arrives at the teaching that Jesus was the Logos, and in the later course of which this beautiful language has all taken shape, represents doctrines which are as unacceptable to us now as they were before; if Jesus' washing of the disciples' feet on the last evening of his life, about which the Synoptics know nothing, remains now, as much as before, something which did not happen; yet the result has been that the working-out of those ideas current amongst Christians of the time which so often took people farther and farther away from the original form of Christianity, leads us back in several main points to its primitive simplicity, and so to what at the present time is the only form that can satisfy us.

12. SPIRITUALISING OF MATERIALISTIC IDEAS.

But the Fourth Gospel is most distinctly modern when it substitutes for the materialistic and literally understood ideas of the earliest Christians, the spiritual interpretations which were already implied in them without people being conscious of the fact. Usually people have no idea how many of the liberal ideas of the present may be found in this Gospel. As regards miracles, we have already decided, that they are only emphatically declared to be real events from one point of view, but that from another standpoint they are regarded purely as symbolical descriptions of profound truths (pp. 95-100, 105 f., 109); and those who are no longer disposed to use them as buttresses of the Christian faith need only appeal to the words which Jesus addressed to Thomas (xx. 29): "blessed are they that have not seen, and yet have believed." The doctrine of the Trinity, which represents that from eternity Father, Son, and Spirit have existed as three divine Persons, and yet only as one divine substance, cannot by any means be maintained in face of Jn.'s statement (vii. 39): "the Spirit did not yet exist, because Jesus was not yet (by his exaltation to heaven) glorified." The belief that prevailed throughout the whole of the first century, that Jesus would come back from heaven to establish the blessed kingdom of the last days, has, in the mind of Jn., resolved itself into the idea that the Holy Spirit, though of course at a quite different time, will come into the hearts of believers. It is all the same to Jn. whether he says that Jesus will come again (xiv. 3, 18, 28; xvi. 22), or that the Holy Spirit will come because God or Jesus will send it (xiv. 16 f., 26; xv. 26; xvi. 7). The Jesus who has been exalted to heaven is for Jn., that is to say, as he was already for Paul (2 Cor. iii. 17), this Spirit; and this again is the reason why the Holy Spirit does not exist before Jesus ascension.

It was generally expected by the early Christians that Jesus second coming from heaven would be the signal for a bodily resurrection and for the judgment to be held before the throne of God upon all mankind; and that eternal life would then begin. In Jn., on the other hand, the judgment takes place during life, when a distinction is drawn between men, and the one section turns towards Jesus, the light which streams upon the world, while the other turns away from him (iii. 19-21). This very moment marks the be ginning of eternal life for such as believe in him or acknowledge God and Jesus; and it is a life which can never be interrupted by the death of the body, and so does not need to be introduced by a resurrection of the body. Compare xi. 25 f.; xvii. 3, and particularly v. 24: "He that heareth my word, and believeth him that sent me, hath eternal life, and cometh not into judgment, but hath passed (already) out of death into life." In fact, participation in the Supper, which according to vi. 51b-56 seems so essential, is made a matter which at bottom is of no importance by the concluding words in vi. 63: "It is the spirit that quickeneth; the flesh profiteth nothing; the words that I have spoken unto you are spirit, and are life." In fact, we can hardly conceive of the matter in a more modern way. And obviously it is not merely the Supper that is stripped of its importance by these words.

13. FINAL APPRECIATION.

We have thus produced ample evidence to show that, although we cannot admit the claim of the Fourth Gospel to be regarded as a record of the life of Jesus, it deserves the highest consideration at the present time when it is viewed as a book dealing with the essence of Christianity. So long as it is read with the idea of finding each particular statement about Jesus' works and discourses to be correct, it cannot be enjoyed. But when this idea is abandoned, and when, in addition, Jesus continual claim upon people to believe in his heavenly origin is set aside, when therefore attention is given only to the thoughts which he is made to express, or when one reads attentively the First Epistle of John, one is impressed by a profundity of thought and feeling, the equal of which cannot easily be found anywhere else in the New Testament.

We may be sure that from the experience of his own soul he knew the value of the benefits offered by religion. He is aware that the religious man has light to illuminate his path (xii. 35), and that he possesses truth--truth which does not merely preserve him from error, but, more than that, delivers him from sin and leads him to holiness (viii. 32-35; xvii. 17-19). He knows of that faith which means resigning one's ego entirely to a higher personality; he knows of that depth of meaning imparted to life which implies that this truly begins at the moment of faith's awakening and cannot be interrupted by the death of the body; he knows of a spring of living water in his soul (iv. 14) and of the true bread from heaven which lasts for the life eternal (vi. 27, 32); he knows of a peace which the world cannot give (xiv. 27; xvi. 33), and of perfect joy (xv. 11; xvii. 13). In a word, he knows what it is to feel oneself a child of God and a friend of one's Master, instead of a slave who does not know what his Master is doing (xv. 14 f.); he knows what it is for a man to feel at one with God and with his Saviour.

For all that constituted his religious aspirations he now found satisfaction in Christianity. But to him this means that he found it in the person of Jesus. For, in addition to all that we have mentioned, he knew something else: that no man has ever seen God, that none can receive any thing unless it be given from heaven, and that one must be chosen and cannot be the chooser of his own Saviour (i. 18; iii. 27; xv. 16). Consequently he needed revelation, and, sharing as he did the ideas of the age in which he lived, he could only conceive of this being imparted by a divine being who came down from heaven, proclaimed all truth, and brought every kind of salvation. The result is he has sketched the Jesus of his own mind in such a way that we men of to-day are often no longer able to find in him the true revelation. And yet in spite of this we can understand the way in which this deeply religious man came to build up this faith of his, In his Gospel we can still discover some very homely statements about Jesus, which show how at first a person's attention might have been attracted to him simply as a remarkable phenomenon: "never man so spake" (vii. 46); "he that speaketh from himself seeketh his own glory, but he that seeketh the glory of him that sent him, the same is true, and no unrighteousness is in him" (vii. 18); "I am the good shepherd: the good shepherd layeth down his life for the sheep" (x. 11). But the author having by such observations as these, which are really appropriate to the historical Jesus, gained confidence in Jesus, his longing for revelation would of itself carry him farther so that he could accept everything else that was recorded of this same Jesus and all those ideas that necessarily seemed to him to be presupposed if in his own person he represented a perfect revelation of God. [10]

This again leads us to the thought that the author of the Fourth Gospel deserves credit for wishing to ascribe to Jesus all the sublime thoughts that he had made his own, especially when we remember that people of other ages, the present not excepted, have in the same way been only too ready to find in Jesus all that at any time has seemed to them truest and best in religion, We can understand now how it is that the author sees in this Jesus, and in him alone, the way to God, the truth and the life (xiv. 6); we can understand the confidence with which he can make him say, "whosoever drinketh of the water that I shall give him shall never thirst" (iv. 14), or "if a man keep my word, he shall never see death" (viii. 51). And one will be glad to be able to say after him, though the words were addressed to another kind of Jesus, "Lord, to whom shall we go? thou hast the words of eternal life" (vi. 68).

At the same time he has not shut his eyes to the truth that Christian knowledge needed to make progress. After the death of Jesus, the Holy Spirit is to guide the disciples into all truth (xvi. 13). We may certainly suppose that the Evangelist himself felt that he was receiving some of this guidance when he advanced so far beyond his predecessors in his effort to spiritualise Christianity. In fact, he has contributed very greatly towards establishing the truth of those words which in his Gospel (iv. 23 f.) Jesus addresses to the woman of Samaria: "the hour cometh and now is (already) when the true worshippers shall worship the Father in spirit and truth . . . God is Spirit, and they that worship him must worship in spirit and truth."

Footnotes:

8. On this see a note by the editor of the present series, and my reply to it, Appendix, pp. 261-269.

9. For further explanation, see Appendix, pp. 270-277.

10. In the suggestion here offered, which of course is not meant to be anything more than a suggestion, we have deliberately assumed that when the Fourth Evangelist devoted himself to Christianity he was of mature age. The growth of his ideas could be explained with very much greater simplicity if we might suppose that he had been educated in Christianity from the days of his youth.

www.ingramcontent.com/pod-product-compliance
Lightning Source LLC
Chambersburg PA
CBHW032050090426
42744CB00004B/154